# TRAPLINE TWINS

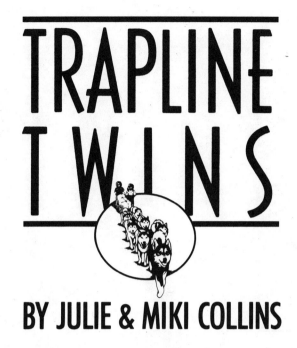

## BY JULIE & MIKI COLLINS

## ALASKA NORTHWEST BOOKS™
A division of GTE Discovery Publications, Inc.

Anchorage • Edmonds

Library of Congress Cataloging - in - Publication Data
Collins, Miki, 1959 -
Trapline Twins
1. Collins, Miki, 1959 -. 2. Collins, Julie, 1959 -.
3. Trappers -- Alaska -- Biography. I. Collins, Julie, 1959 -. II. Title.
SK17.C58A3 1989 639'.1'0922 [B] 88-34231
ISBN 0-88240-332-X


Design by Virginia Hance
Photos by Julie and Miki Collins
Alaska Northwest Books™
A division of GTE Discovery Publications Inc.
130 Second Avenue South
Edmonds, Washington 98020
Printed in U.S.A.

# CONTENTS

| Chapter | | Page |
|---|---|---|
| | Preface | V |
| 1 | Trial Run | 1 |
| 2 | A Good Start | 9 |
| 3 | First Days on the Trapline | 21 |
| 4 | The Way of Life | 38 |
| 5 | Trapline Traveler | 56 |
| 6 | The Birds and the Bees and the Bears | 74 |
| 7 | Moose, More Bears and Rotten Ice | 94 |
| 8 | A Flying Family | 130 |
| 9 | Dogs | 144 |
| 10 | Dog-Team Holiday | 163 |
| 11 | Bad Start, Bad Finish | 180 |
| 12 | The Yukon Quest | 197 |
| 13 | Trails to the Future | 209 |

# PREFACE

This is an adventure book. It is not a how-to book, nor does it glorify trapping nor the bush Alaska way of life. It is a book about how we live, our trials and tribulations, triumphs and disasters.

For three years we struggled with the idea of writing this book. We didn't really want to display our precious lifestyle in a permanent form, possibly encouraging others to seek it for themselves when wilderness resources are already stretched, when recent state and federal land sales have threatened us with the problem now menacing many of earth's creatures — loss of habitat. Unlike many writers who chronicle their Alaskan experiences, we have not moved on to other lives and occupations. We *live* in the bush. We *are* trappers. Our adventures are still happening. Many — some of the best — will have to wait for Book Two.

But write it we did, with trepidation and the fervent hope that Our Readers will respect our lives and our valued privacy. Here are some of our favorite adventure stories — chasing a grizzly bear with a dog team, falling through ice, struggling with overflow and cold and exhaustion on the trapline, running sled-dog races; dog stories, puppy stories and trail stories.

Because we both wrote this book, each taking certain chapters, you may be confused now and again. Did Miki shoot that big bull moose, or was it Julie? But don't worry; since we're identical twins, most everyone around us lives in a state of perpetual confusion. If Miki hadn't shot a moose that year, Julie would have, so it really doesn't matter. We each answer to either name anyway.

This way of life is rare today, and dying out as Civilization approaches. We do not take our good fortune for granted, and if we seem selfish for not wanting to share anything beyond the stories our life produces, it is only because we value our lifestyle so much. To share it is to lose it. An eight-hundred-square-mile trapline can support two trappers if handled properly, but no more. But with stories, we can be generous! It has been our privilege to live this life, and now it is our privilege to share it with you.

*Dedication*

To Daddy and Marmee,
who supported us in the path we chose to follow, and to
our brother, Ray,
who pointed out the trail.

*Acknowledgments*

Some stories in this book appeared in different form
in periodicals including *Alaska*,
the *Fairbanks Daily News-Miner*, *Northland News*,
*Alaskafest*, *Alaska Airlines Magazine* and *Alaska Gangline*.
Parts of chapters three and six appeared in different form in
*Sports Afield*, January 1982 and 1985 Hunting Edition.
Parts of chapters three and five appeared in
*Fur-Fish-Game*, December 1982 and March 1984.
All appear here with permission from the original publishers.

# 1

# TRIAL RUN

I stood at the crest of a mountainous snowdrift and looked down from the wind-shaped cornice at the road that emerged from the snow far below me.

"How does it look?" my twin sister asked anxiously.

"We've got about thirty feet of vertical snow," I answered. Miki's hazel eyes widened with surprise. "With a six-foot cornice at the top," I added.

"Can we get the dogs down it?"

I eyed the small trail sled loaded with camping gear, the eight huskies waiting in their harnesses, and my twin sister standing on the runners waiting for my decision. "I don't know, but we're going to try. I don't think we can get around it, and we can't really go back, can we?"

Behind us the deserted, snow-drifted road wound

through mountain passes to the headquarters of Denali National Park. Ahead lay the hazards of the Alaska bush, but deep in that land, beyond an unfamiliar stretch of mountains, was our home. That's where we were going — home. For nine winters we had struggled with school in Fairbanks, but we were finally ready to be graduated from college. During our spring break, before the last of the snow melted, we wanted to mush our dogs to our isolated bush village to avoid the cost of flying them home later.

Our excitement was heightened by just a touch of fear as we turned our big wheel dogs loose from their places in front of the sled. With the light wooden craft free-falling down that monster snowdrift, we didn't want it running over the dogs in front of it.

Miki held the alert team back as I leaped over the cornice and plunged fifteen feet down to where the slope grew less steep. I slid to the bottom, then turned and shouted to the dogs.

"OK, let's go!"

Our two gutsy leaders, Tonto and King, jumped boldly over the crest, dragging the other dogs behind them. The team cascaded down the snow cliff, and then Miki and her sled flew over the edge. She plummeted downward, losing control of the sled near the bottom as it skidded up on the dogs. At the road below, she snapped the sled straight and stopped the team.

Another obstacle behind us. Already we had traveled along gravel roads, on river ice and glazed creeks, and tundra laid bare by an early spring. The sled brake, already battered by exposed tundra tussocks, had broken and been temporarily lashed back into place. The rough going had also broken one of our skis while Miki was skijoring behind the sled, making travel all the more tedious. Despite the troubles we kept on, determined to reach home.

Ever since we put together a dog team at age fifteen, we had dreamed of mushing our dogs from Fairbanks to our lifelong home at Lake Minchumina. This ten-day spring break shortly before graduation was our last chance. We planned to move home permanently in May. The vacation came in late March and an early breakup meant tough going, but we decided to try it. We knew this wouldn't be a pleasure trip, but at the time we had only a little cross-country work behind us and we didn't realize just how much could go wrong.

Now the trail wound up and around Stony Hill, stretching out toward the great mountain, Denali. We toiled steadily upward, one struggling with the broken ski while the other struggled with the loaded sled as it dragged heavily across patches of gravel.

"I think — I think we've come too far," Miki said at last as we stopped to study the map and rest the dogs. "We should've left the road two miles back and dropped down the valley into Thorofare Creek."

I studied the craggy white mountains, with Denali above them all in a curtain of clouds. Below us lay a vast glacial flood plain, the level whiteness broken and spotted by rocky cobblestones. The road stretched ahead of us, inviting us to continue above the valley, but it was leading us up the side of a mountain. To reach the valley we had to go three hundred feet down — almost straight down.

We decided, as usual, to go the hard and fast way rather than backtracking to a safer route down. We intended to follow a sloping shoulder part way before dropping down to a steep, narrow ravine into a gorge which led to the valley. We left the road and jolted over the tundra to a treacherous drop-off just above the narrow ravine. I volunteered to drive the sled down this first plunge. It looked too dangerous to take the whole team down, so we unhooked most of the dogs and let them run loose. The sled darted forward, gaining momentum as I gripped the handlebow.

We skidded over an icy bank and, as the ground dropped away, my light craft became airborne, shooting over the tundra and arching gracefully downward. It crashed nose-first into the frozen ground.

I spun away from the sled, my grip broken by the impact. The sled skidded and rolled, and I bounced and rolled, then bounced some more before jamming in the frozen tussocks. After lying in the hummocks for awhile I decided to at least try to get up, so Miki would know I was alive. Feeling myself tenderly, I discovered to my astonishment that only my eyeglasses were broken. The sled looked all right, too. Later we realized that the right runner must have been cracked.

"*You* can take it down that gully," I said. "I'm not going down any more hills."

Miki studied the steep little ravine leading into the gorge below. "Why don't *you* go over there and make sure there isn't a frozen waterfall under that snow?"

I walked to the precipice and started down. One foot slipped and without warning I was sliding downward in ice cleverly hidden under a half-inch of snow. Luckily I skidded to a stop on a patch of gravel, and then inched my way down. The entire ravine lay coated with ice.

"We can't go down there," I told Miki.

"We jolly well have to."

"We can't!"

"We *have* to!"

"Well — how about lowering the sled down backward with the towline?"

"OK."

We turned the dogs loose again and Miki guided the sled from below as I walked it down with the long towline.

Two-thirds of the way down I slipped on the ice and the rope snapped away. Miki and the sled glided helplessly to the bottom of the icy ravine, twisting in graceful pirouettes as they slid over bumps and dips.

I brought the dogs down while Miki scouted the last descent. "We're going to rough-lock it this time," she declared grimly.

We wrapped twenty-five pounds of stake-out chain around the runners, but even with the added friction Miki had only a vestige of control, and one railing snapped as the sled ploughed past some thick willows.

Dusk was falling when we broke out onto the wide flood plain. This was no place to camp, with neither a tree for shelter nor a twig for fire. I jogged ahead of the dogs, guiding them across the trackless, rocky ground. After four long miles over the cobbles, Thorofare Creek narrowed into a low canyon. That's where our troubles began.

Two inches of ice had formed over the creek, and the underlying water had later drained away, leaving a hollow shell. The dogs trotted easily over it, but again and again the sled broke through and tumbled two feet down to the boulder-strewn creek bottom. Despite the bad ice we were clipping along fairly well until the sled crashed down again, this time slamming to a halt so violent it threw me from my perch atop the load. Miki dived forward to see what the trouble was, and came up swearing to the best of her very limited ability.

"We've busted a runner!"

Short of total disintegration, a broken runner is the most serious accident a sled can have. The right runner, probably damaged in the earlier crash, had snapped in front of the first upright stanchion. When we tried to move, the jagged edge plowed us to halt.

I ran down the creek to see whether the canyon opened

up soon onto the McKinley River, where we could find spruce trees to camp in. The  valley twisted on forever and I returned in despair.

"We're in big trouble," I said.

"We'll never get out of here by dark," Miki added gloomily.

"We can't camp here. There's nothing here, no spruce boughs to sleep on or anything."

"I don't think we've got much choice," Miki said.

A narrow sandbar lay jammed between the boulders of the creek and the gravelly cliffs above us, and we ferried our load up there, dragged the crippled sled over, and set up camp. The darkness in the canyon made our troubles seem all the more oppressive. Back in those rough old days we traveled cheaply, without air mattresses, headlamps or the newer, light-weight cable pickets for the dogs. Miki slept in the sled, as usual, but without the comfort of a soft spruce-bough mattress under me, I lay awake for some time on a skimpy mattress of dog-food sacks and a couple of burlap sacks on the snow. I lay awake thinking until I figured out how to repair the runner with no spare lumber nor even a tree to hack out a splint.

With the new day came renewed determination, and as the sun rose over the rim of the canyon, my spirits lifted. While Miki dried our frost-dampened gear over a willow-twig fire, I fastened the broken ski against the broken sled runner as a splint and lashed the works together with all the twine we had.

We were on the way again, dodging boulders and skidding around icy turns. Then, stopping to check the route ahead, we found bear tracks in the snow. Grizzly tracks. Fresh.

"He's somewhere ahead of us," I said, my heart pounding. Spring bears can be ornery.

"The only direction we can go is downriver," Miki replied. "We sure can't get out of this canyon any other way."

"Right." We hiked up the dogs and went on cautiously, every nerve taut. If the canyon didn't open up soon, we were likely to run up on the bear. Those tracks had been made since the last afternoon's thaw.

Soon eight pairs of ears pricked up and the dogs slammed into their harnesses in unison. The scent of bear changed them from steady workers to stampeding maniacs, and on the glare ice I couldn't check their charge.

A great shadow undulated beyond the cover of thick willows one hundred and fifty yards away. "There he is," I gasped. The dogs went crazy.

"Look out for those rocks! You'll smash that bad runner!" Miki yelled.

"*You* watch for the bear, *I'm* driving the sled!" I shouted back. Miki clung tight to the top of the load as we careened toward the boulders. At the last instant I skidded the sled sideways so the strong left runner absorbed the impact as we crashed and shuddered to a halt.

"Settle down, boys," I growled at the dogs, glancing warily toward where I had last glimpsed the grizzly. We lined out the tangled huskies and they surged forward again, still loping but less frantically. We chased the bear, or rather his tracks, for two miles. Just as the canyon began to open up we saw him again, far ahead of us. Miki grabbed a tin can and banged loudly on it. The grizzly spun around, lifting his head. He stared at us and we stared back. Miki quietly put the can down.

The dogs were rapidly closing the distance between us, and we weren't sure whether the bear would run or charge, but with the broken sled brake skittering over the glazed ice, it was impossible to stop the driving team. Finally the bear turned away, heading for a ravine leading up the canyon wall. We didn't see him again.

The valley widened and the creek opened up on broad flats littered with open channels and cobblestones. Wading the numerous ice-water streams soon soaked our boots, socks and feet, but we kept on, always hoping for better conditions ahead. After fighting our way down the McKinley River for a day, we cut cross-country and ran into deep snow.

Snow cliffs, bare trails, treacherous mountainsides, open water and the grizzly had failed to stop us, but the deep snow did. Four feet of it, heavy with meltwater and almost impossible to snowshoe in, the thick slush slowed our pace to a crawl. With the dogs growing ever more weary, our gear suffering from the abuse, and the broken runner dragging, we covered only twelve miles in three days.

We were out of dog food, school started in just a couple of days, and we were still more than sixty miles from home. Reluctantly we flagged down our brother, Ray, when he flew over in a ski plane to check on us. We cached the sled in the trees, and four hours later, after three round trips with the Supercub to ferry our dogs and gear, we were home.

We had failed to reach our destination unaided, and the defeat stung. Later we realized that the worst adventures make for the best memories. Although in the years to come we were to log thousands of miles in cross-country dogsled trips, that hundred-mile adventure ranks at the top for pure excitement.

Anyway, the dogs were home and that was our main goal. After another month of school we would be home too, home to stay.

# A GOOD START

Our father, Richard Collins, came north in 1942 to work on the Alaska Highway. He then worked for twenty-five years in the bush for the Federal Aviation Administration. When they transferred him to Lake Minchumina, he stayed with the Flight Service Station there until they tried to transfer him to Anchorage. Then he retired.

Our mother, Florence Rucker, drove the Alaska Highway in 1948 with a girlfriend, also named Florence. After they discovered the difficulty of traveling in a land without roads, Marmee, as we call her, and Florence bought a little Cessna 140. In the next few years they flew across Alaska for pleasure and in connection with their work as geologists.

The 85-horse airplane gave questionable performance on Alaska's improvised bush strips, and when the two returned to the States later they purchased a Supercub on floats. They flew across the continent together, from Washington, D.C., to the Mackenzie River Delta on the Canadian Arctic Ocean, and on to Fairbanks at a time when planes in the Far North were still something special, and women pilots were almost unheard of. ("Look! An Airplane! Oh — oh, look! *Girls!*")

In 1956, Florence Rucker and Florence Robinson (known as Ru and Ro) landed at Lake Minchumina, and one year later it was Marmee's home. Daddy jokes that he really wanted the Supercub on floats, but in striking the deal he happily threw in the best husband and father a family could ask for. He wasn't even too upset when the beloved old plane was wrecked two decades later.

Our early years spent at the FAA housing weren't much unlike other children's lives. We played on the lawn and swing sets, rode tricycles and bikes, and watched monthly movies imported by the FAA. When other families moved in for a few months, Marmee made us play with the children. Later, when Daddy retired, we moved across the lake to an old place that was once a fur farm.

We had one old neighbor, Slim Carlson, who left during the winters to run his trapline with his big old huskies. Slim was an institution at our village, and I admired him so much I was scared to talk to him very often.

Our days passed in youthful bliss. We played in the forest, on the mud flats across the bay, in the lake. We helped (and hindered) our parents as they brought logs in by raft and bobsled and built a new home. We had a lot of fun growing up there with our older brother, Ray, and for all the hard playing we did we almost never got into trouble.

But one warm summer day Miki was attacked in our strawberry patch. We had gone out early in the morning to pick some sweet, half-wild berries for breakfast and our bowls were almost full when Miki noticed a small movement nearby.

"Look!" she cried. "A little brown bird under Daddy's trailer! No, it's an animal, it's a weasel, and — oh, he's after me!" With a shriek she threw up her hands, sending her little plastic bowl of berries spinning away like a frisbee, ripe strawberries spewing in all directions.

The weasel, in his summer coat of soft brown and yellow, rushed straight at her and seized the hem of her pajamas. Miki managed to kick him away and flew home, the tiny vicious creature hot on her heels. He narrowly escaped being crushed as the cabin door slammed, leaving Miki safe and unhurt inside. Meantime I went running and screaming for help, and eventually Ray found the insane weasel and shot him. He must have had rabies or some other form of dementia, to have gone mad like that.

As we grew older Marmee taught us to cook and clean, to knit and to sew with cloth, fur and leather, and to preserve the meat, berries and garden vegetables we gathered from the land. There was no school, so she taught us herself with correspondence courses from the state. From her we inherited a passion for reading, and later, for writing.

Later, Daddy taught us to pilot a plane, drive motorboats and snow machines, and run the chain saw, water pumps and diesel generator. Unfortunately we never figured out how to repair any of them when they broke down, and "Daddy will fix it" has been our motto for many years. Many's the time Miki and I have rowed our little flat-bottomed boat home when a simple repair job might have got the old outboard running again.

Daddy fixed up our home with solar, wind and diesel power, a battery-operated freezer, solar water heater and ham radio communications, and he soon had us running them too.

With electricity, running water (combined with an outhouse) and a wood-burning barrel furnace, we have a modern home, yet it's easily shut down when the folks go on their two-month vacations, leaving Miki and me to stay in the smaller, simpler cabin next door.

Ray, a year and a half older, taught Miki and me about the land, its kindness and its cruelty. We had to learn it from him, but he didn't learn from anybody. He simply absorbed it. As a youngster he brought home voles and rabbits, a baby squirrel and once a fox kit. All of them caused trouble. The voles perpetuated themselves, and their countless offspring escaped to infest our cabin. The hares became tame and then domineering. They won wrestling matches with the house dog, chewed electrical cords and left rabbit pellets in the farthest corners. When we petted them, they'd nibble and lick our arms gently, but after cleaning off a spot they'd chomp down to draw blood.

The fox made a general nuisance of himself until he was evicted. The squirrel, Oliver (so named because he came home in an old olive can), hid insulation and graham crackers in our antique clock, chattered in the early-morning hours, and later ran away with a lady friend, never to return. His progeny came back, though, to invade three old cabins, two caches and the dog-food shed.

Ray was a Master Catcher. He grabbed rabbits as they sped past, he grabbed spruce hens in the forest and he grabbed ducks in the marsh. He caught a marten in a hand-held snare while both swung from the top of a spruce tree. He stalked moose without a weapon; he got treed once, but continued the sport undaunted. He once captured a bald eagle in his bare hands, and he snatched a swallow in flight as it swooped past him.

Ray taught us to shoot, set snares and traps, gut a

moose and distinguish ducks, geese and loons in flight. Once he led a wolf pack along a riverbank to us and we watched, enchanted, as the great animals approached to fifteen feet and answered our inviting howls with a chorus of their own.

One day when we were far from home he got hungry, caught a frog, drowned it, and swallowed it whole, partly to impress his bug-eyed sisters. Then he turned pale. "I'm not sure it was dead," he told us weakly.

Ray was an incorrigible schemer and he usually sold us on his marvelous ideas. One plan was an infallible method of catching muskrats, and as the pelts were valuable to kids on a fifty-cents-a-week allowance, Miki and I willingly came along.

"Now, we cut off the tops of the muskrat pushups in the ice, and when a 'rat comes out to eat his dinner, we take our sticks and *wham*! Bash his head in. We'll each stake out a pushup so we'll be sure not to miss any. Piece of cake."

I sat on the ice beside the pile of weeds that made up the muskrat's winter feeding lodge. I sat there with my stick until my feet went numb clear to my knees. Then — up popped a muskrat.

*Wham*!

The little beggar was gone before I even started the swing. Miki and Ray dashed over, excitement running high.

"Let's go home," I said.

Well, maybe that wasn't such a good idea. But we learned.

Ray took us out ice-skating on sparkling moonlit nights when the lake ice froze smooth and glassy. We picked cattails, soaked them in diesel fuel, and lit them as torches. Skimming across the black ice, we followed the reflected white path of the moon in the heavens. The ice lay speckled with small and large white shell-like bubbles of methane gas, trapped under films of frozen water. The spots signaled weak ice and we'd swing wide, but when we found a big bubble we'd circle back to examine it.

Ray always took the lead. If the bubble looked good, he'd kneel beside it and tap a tiny hole through the ice over the bubble. As water pressure forced the swamp gas out, Ray's cattail torch swept down to light the gas. With a soft *whoomp*, an ephemeral blue flame would burst up from the frozen lake, sometimes a few inches and sometimes three feet high.

We'd spend the dark evenings skating and searching for bubbles to light. Sometimes the methane exploded from the hole in half a second and sometimes it lasted half a minute, the blue and white and yellow light blindingly beautiful in the black night.

Once we came across a bubble four feet across with several more chambers of gas frozen around it. This would be spectacular! Eagerly we crowded around, looking for the best spot to break the ice.

"Get back!" Ray warned dramatically. "It could blow sky-high." Miki and I retreated upwind of the bubble as Ray held his torch ready and lightly kicked the fragile shell ice with the pointed heel of his skate.

The gas exploded from the hole, flames roaring six feet high. For some seconds we watched, speechless, as the blue flame blazed upward until it withered, sank back to the hole, and popped out with a burble of water.

Ray tottered to his feet, eyes red and watering, his shaggy brown hair singed, while Miki and I gazed at him with awe.

We still go out on the bay in the fall when the ice freezes smooth as glass, and we still light methane bubbles when we find them, but never again have I seen a flame like that one.

If Ray was our mentor, Slim Carlson was our idol. Slim

came to Alaska from Sweden in the early part of the century, and began trapping the wilderness north of Denali around 1918. He lived off the land, traveling by dog team along hundreds of miles of trails he cleared himself, back in the days when there was wilderness enough for everyone.

Slim was a powerful man, a mountain of a man. When a line cabin burned down, stranding him in long johns without boots, he survived the dogsled trip fifteen miles back to another cabin. When his toes froze and turned gangrenous, he whittled them off. When in a single careless moment he accidentally chopped off his thumb, hundreds of miles from any doctor, he nursed the stump himself.

When the time came for him to die, Slim faced it with the same quiet courage. Instead of withering away as many old people do, when Slim sensed his life was over he simply stopped eating and so ended his life with dignity.

Slim left us a legacy of which I have always been proud. He gave his trapline to us, and when Ray moved away after school Miki and I took over most of it. But Slim left us more than trapping rights to a great piece of land rich in marten, fox and lynx. He left more than his traps, cabins and trapping gear.

He left us with a sense of responsibility, a sense of pride in our legacy, a feeling of loyalty to him and to the land he had worked on and loved for more than half a century. We felt the necessity to restore his dilapidated cabins, clear the overgrown trails, and trap the lines as he did — on foot and by dog team, not with overpowered snow machines and all-terrain vehicles. We take his work seriously, tend our traps and pelts with great care, and take pride in our chores, for to fail in them, or to perform them shabbily, would be to fail the greatest man I ever knew.

The old Swede died at eighty-nine when Miki and I were fifteen. In his advancing years he had been unable to maintain the trapline. The cabins were caving in, traps rusting and cubbies tumbling down. It would be a tremendous job to restore the entire line, with more than two hundred miles of trail, to its original state. But eager as we were, the work had to be put off for nine long years. While the old trails slowly sank into the forest, Miki and I left the bush to face the greatest challenge of our life. Fairbanks.

Daddy and Marmee wanted us to experience the formal school system and have the advantage of its facilities — the chemicals to mix, animals to dissect, field trips, gym equipment, teachers who specialized in areas like literature and biology. They wanted to prepare us for college, and they knew we had to learn to get along with our fellow human beings.

Rather than board us with strangers in town, as most bush parents must, they built a house in Fairbanks and lived there during the years we were in school.

At home, taking correspondence courses, there were no bells to tell us when to start and stop, and a few minutes more or less didn't matter. We moved from one lesson to the next as each was completed. If we had trouble with one subject we spent more time on it, and if it was easy we moved fast. If we worked on a Saturday, we earned an extra day off the following weekend.

The routine of school was rigid: catch the school bus, get to class, get to roll call and lectures, all at specified times. Making good grades was no problem. Marmee, with her college background, had prepared us well academically and the course work was so basic that we rarely had to study. With the enforced schedules and lack of challenge, we grew bored and apathetic. But that didn't bother us so much as the kids. Marmee could not have prepared us for them. The kids swarmed the halls, shoving and yelling and swearing, even when the teachers told them to be quiet. We'd been reared to respect and obey our elders, and such unruliness shocked us. We didn't understand the kids and they didn't understand us. At an age when each one felt the importance of being individual, different, Miki and I were too different. We were quiet, terribly shy, and prime targets for malicious merriment.

Yet I was glad to be different. I felt superior because I came from the bush. I had learned responsibility, and I wasn't about to lower myself to screaming in the halls. We shunned the kids, even the friendly ones.

For the first two years we had Kathy, the girl next door, who became a faithful companion and helped us out when we got stuck socially. After she moved away we simply didn't make other close friends. We had each other, and we were adjusted to the bizarre life. About that time, too, we started picking up sled dogs at the rate of one or two a year, as many as our parents would tolerate, and we turned to our dogs for entertainment and companionship.

For the first three years, the hardest years, I kept a calendar in my notebook, and every single day during the first class, I blacked out the day before. I didn't cross it off, I blacked it out. I wanted it to vanish, to be forgotten forever.

As I look back I still feel the pain, but I feel no resentment toward my parents, and I didn't then. I understood their motives, and I knew they were making sacrifices for us. They disliked town life as much as we did. Especially Daddy. Every weekend when the weather was flyable, he'd bundle us into his Cessna 180 and fly us home for two glorious days. That took money and effort, but he never let us down. He wanted to escape almost as much as we did.

By the time we finished high school, Miki and I had overcome our shyness fairly well and were able to face four years at the university.

Being identical twins does get awkward sometimes.

You have to put up with the same conversations over and over with different people, who think they are being witty. Most of them go like this:

"You two aren't sisters, are you?"

We grin sheepishly and both answer, "Yeah."

"Twins?"

A fleeting exchange of glances and another simultaneous "Yeah."

"Wow, neat! Identical?"

"Yeah" again.

Conversations with acquaintances are predictable, too. They start out, "Are you Miki or Julie? Don't tell me, let me guess." Much squinting and jaw-rubbing, and then, "Miki?"

"You were close," I'll say. "It doesn't matter, anyway. I answer to either name."

Then came the time someone said, "Let me guess. Miki?" And I automatically replied, "Yeah, I mean . . . wait a minute! Which one am I, anyway?"

We aren't exactly the same, of course — both a little short and stubby, same snub nose, glasses and dirty blond hair, but our brother Ray can tell us apart at a glance and our parents almost always can. Our grandmother never could, but as I said before, it doesn't really matter. We both answer to either name.

Well, sometimes it matters a little. Like the time back in school a stranger called to me, "Hi, Miki!"

"Hi," I replied, grinning brightly.

"How'd you do on the psych exam?"

Oh-oh! I wasn't taking psychology. "All right, I guess," I replied warily.

"How'd you like that last essay question?"

"Not bad, I guess. Nice to see you," and I hurried away.

It's not nice to fool people, but it saves hassle for us all.

Of course people often suggest we trade places if one is better at something than the other, like applying for a license, taking an exam or running a dogsled race. The only time we ever deliberately impersonated each other was in high-school Spanish class. I sat in Miki's desk, she sat in mine; I answered the questions Miss Peters directed at Miki, and she answered for me. We didn't get caught, and it wasn't a bit of fun.

Then there is the rare occasion when we don't want to be even distantly related. A few years ago, on a very crowded afternoon at O'Hare Airport in Chicago, I set off the metal detector, and a frenzied officer found a .308 shell in my jeans pocket. I'd left it there after a bear hunt a couple of weeks earlier, to impress by Stateside cousins. During the ensuing turmoil Miki stood with her back turned, gazing out the window, so no one would notice she was my mirror image.

It can get embarrassing, too, like when I lose Miki in the huge J.C. Penney store in Fairbanks. I'll look and look, and suddenly spot her nearby. Then I wave and give a little shout to attact her attention, only to discover I'm waving and shouting at my own reflection in a full-length mirror.

We never had any serious romances during those nine school years in town, partly, I suppose, because we clung so tightly to each other, and partly because we were so bashful. At home, we're so busy and so isolated we've never made any close friends. We do worry, though, about the consequences if one of us should come home from town with an awe-struck expression and whisper, "I found a man!"

Those who've known us the longest don't seem to mind which one they're talking to. "Miki-Julie," says Postmaster Mary Flood without even glancing up. Even if I'm there alone it's "Miki-Julie." It saves a great deal of confusion. "The Twinnies," says Hazel Menke, our neighbor who used to baby-sit us some twenty years ago.

Having a twin means having a partner I can work with and understand. We may fight over who gets to fly the plane this time, or shoot the moose this fall, or wash the dishes or pick up the dog yard, but our spats are short-lived and soon forgotten.

But the best part is sharing. A sense of humor doesn't go far unless another person laughs with you. When I'm spending time alone on the trapline, it's the shared laughter I miss most.

Hazel Menke put it all together the year she sent us a Christmas card with two little Indian children sleeping peacefully against a wall. That card is still nailed up in one of our line cabins, and if you open it you can read the inscription:

"To have joy one must share it. Happiness was born a twin."

# 3

# FIRST DAYS
# ON THE TRAPLINE

"I say, it *is* cold," I observed as Julie rushed back into the little Igloo Creek cabin, a great gush of cold steam swirling after her. She leaned the disconnected door back in place and plopped down on the snowdrift next to the roaring, leaking half-drum stove.

"Yeah, I wish we were at the Birch Cabin right now!"

Julie and I had taken a full day to break out those seven miles of trail now behind us, snowshoeing ahead of the dog team through two feet of fresh snow as the clear sky sucked away the warmth lingering from that last weather front. Now, in the darkness of the early January evening, the temperature sank lower still. We holed up in this tiny, decrepit line cabin, throwing a sled tarp over the half of the roof that was caved in, and tied the dogs outside where they curled into tight balls of frosty fur against the cold, tails over their noses.

Julie and I had been "trapping" ever since we were old enough to tag along after our brother when he ran his rabbit snares as a youngster, but this was our first real attempt and we had a lot more lessons ahead of us than behind. After Ray had graduated from high school he spent a year trapping, and on vacations Julie and I joined him, eager to get away from school. During those brief episodes we learned the rudiments of trapping: how to build a marten cubby with spruce boughs, how to snare a beaver through three feet of ice, and how it felt to walk twenty-three miles behind a dogsled, traveling for thirteen hours, from pre-dawn until long after dark. And that was about the extent of our trapping know-how.

Then we were all three off to college, limiting our trapping adventures to a few weekends pinching muskrat paws near home. But when Julie and I had saved up enough credit at the University of Alaska to take one semester off and still graduate in four years, we went home to try a little serious trapping.

We flew home in mid-December, jam-packing the Piper Navajo mail plane with eight burly huskies and our long freight sled. On Christmas Day we spent the afternoon whizzing through the shallow snow for thirteen miles up the winter trail up a twisting, frozen marshy creek, and returned home triumphantly in time for dinner.

Then it turned cold. Forty below cold. It warmed up again long enough to dump two feet of snow. As soon as that was over we headed out again while the cold settled in once more. Instead of whizzing we trudged on snowshoes, sometimes covering the trail back and forth twice before the team could pull the loaded sled through the powder. River ice sagged and cracked under the new load, letting overflow ooze up to freeze onto the sled runners, and time and again we had to beat off the freezing slush with the ax. Finally, long after dark, we reached the half-fallen-in Igloo Creek cabin and holed up on that cold, dark night.

For another day we plodded onward, turning around just after dark and fleeing back to the little hovel for another chilly night. The rotting logs sported holes big enough to stick a fist through, the door was off the hinges, and the sled tarp over the remains of the roof did little to keep in the small amount of heat we coaxed from the sullen stove. Having neither time nor energy to cut much wood, we let the fire die shortly after crawling into our heavy sleeping bags, and in an hour or two the cabin temperature dropped nearly to that outside. In the two nights we spent there the snowdrift on the floor never melted more than a foot back from the stove.

Daddy came out by snow machine the following morning to check up on us. I crawled out the low doorway as he pulled up, parka hood low around his grinning face.

"Guess how cold it is," he said, shutting off the chugging engine.

"Thirty below," I offered cautiously.

"Fifty below! It hasn't been above forty-five below since the day you left!"

That cold weather hung around for weeks, staying between forty and fifty below during the last part of December and a good bit of January, except for the short periods of warmth which brought the snow swirling maliciously down to cover and recover our trail. It was too cold to go far and Julie and I spent a lot of time hunting rabbits — snowshoe hares — to feed the dogs. We set a net under the ice, but the fish don't move much that time of year and we sure didn't catch many.

When the weather warmed up a little we headed out the trail on snowshoes, leaving the dogs behind. We left at seven a.m. and spent eleven hours snowshoeing out the inundated trail, traveling about twenty miles round-trip. I'd never snow-shoed that far before in my life, and even though we could take turns breaking trail and had a good return path, we were hurting by the time we reached the shore below the house.

"Let's spend the night under the fish rack," I joked. "I can't make it up the hill!"

But we did stagger up the hill, that time and many more times before we finally reached the Birch Cabin eighteen miles away. Several days of February had come and gone by then, but with eighteen miles of traps and snares set we began catching fur, not much, but regularly — about two marten a week.

This trapline has been in use since the early 1900s. When Mount McKinley (now Denali) National Park was established the trappers were forced out, and Slim Carlson, who had been doing a little mining and trapping in the area southwest of Wonder Lake, moved over and bought out another trapper, Gus Johnson, in about 1922. He cut more trail, covering a wide area until he had more than two hundred miles of line. Of that, he regularly trapped perhaps one hundred miles each year. When he was in his sixties people began to worry about him, and at their urging he moved closer to civilization, to a small cabin near the homestead which Marmee bought later. He was still trapping ten years later, when we were little kids. We admired him no end, and we adored his big, old scarred huskies.

Although he had an ancient outboard motor which he used when traveling farther than the rowing distance to his fishnet, he never used a snow machine and he never used a chain saw. Sometimes Daddy or other bush pilots flew fish for his dogs to the farthest reaches of his trapline, but for the most part he did everything for himself. When he was about seventy-seven he built the eighteen-by-twenty-four log cabin next to our place, and except for help hauling out the logs and raising the ridgepole, he wouldn't let a soul join the work. "Aye vant it done my vay," he said, and that's exactly the way it was done.

He trapped a one-hundred-mile line into his seventies, gradually cutting back until his last run in his eighties. When he died a few years later he left everything to Daddy who, not being a trapper, handed the line over to the next generation. Although Ray traps on and off, Julie and I took it on as a full-time job.

That first year we didn't know what we were doing and I marvel that we caught anything at all. Our parents headed south in January for their annual two-month vacation, and we moved next door into Slim's one-room cabin where we would not have to worry about water pipes freezing or the generator breaking down. We slipped easily into a routine, spending two or three days a week on the trapline and hunting small game and running the fishnet when we were at the lake. Sometimes one of us skied to the Birch Cabin, and the other followed the next day with the team and a load of freight — mostly dog food. We toughened up enough to make the eighteen-mile ski easily. Our team also hardened in response to the poor trail conditions, and could make the run with energy to spare. February and March brought mild temperatures, often well above zero, and our faces turned brown from long days spent on the trail.

The best times were at the Birch Cabin. The tiny log cabin stands on the edge of a creek in a cluster of tall white spruce and birch, and from the river front we can see Denali towering above the surrounding timber. During the dark days of midwinter, in the pale pre-dawn interval just before the sun peeps over the crest of the mountain, we are truly in the Shadow of Denali.

I thought of Slim often during those learning days, seeing again his tall frame topped by a shock of snowy hair, powerful even at eighty-five. He'd said he had spent most of his years beneath McKinley and figured he'd leave his bones in its shadow. He did, too. Daddy flew his ashes to Lonely Lake, fifty miles out on his trapline, where the mountain towers above everything, only twenty miles away and more than four miles high. I wished Slim were still here, to share the knowledge he had gained during his sixty years alone with his dogs in the depths of the wilderness.

Slim is the only person I ever truly idolized. He had more integrity than anyone that I have ever known; he had the confidence to do what he wanted, and the honesty and the pride to do it right. Even today, as Julie and I trap this line, living in cabins which did not exist when he was alive and clearing trails unused for twenty years or more, I feel it is not ours; it belongs to him, we are only borrowing it, and we must take care of the land and everything in it the best way we know how.

That first spring on the trapline taught us a lot. The knowledge was wrested from experiences, by trial and error. We made up our own trapping tactics and were delighted at any success, no matter how meager. We melted lake ice for drinking water, washed clothes in an old fish tub, and lived richly on moose, ptarmigan, grouse and garden vegetables in addition to the array of store-bought goods our folks left us. For the most part we lived alone, seeing people only on the weekly mail day when we mushed the six miles across the lake to meet the mail plane. Being on the reticent side, this suited us just fine. I remember only two visits in three months; two guys who stopped to dry off after soaking their feet in overflow down-river, and the census-taker!

When the trail was good the run to the Birch Cabin took less than three hours by dog team, and Julie once skied it in three and a half hours. But we were not always so lucky. Julie made the trip once during a wind storm with gusts registering up to sixty-three miles an hour. Later that same day, after snowshoeing on out the line, she started back across the creek near the cabin, only to leap back just as her weight caused a fifteen-foot section of ice to cave into the dark, swirling water.

Then, on the last run of the year, we ran into trouble with breakup. We were pulling out after beaver-trapping in early April and every day brought sunshine, temperatures in the forties, a little less snow and a little more water.

Even at four-thirty a.m. the sky showed light, but two hours slipped by as we cached the nonperishable food and prepared to leave the cabin, hoping to reach home before the heat of day turned the trail to slush. Ray's trapping partner, Jeff Coe, had joined us earlier in the spring to go after beaver, and he showed us how to tie a gee pole to the heavily loaded sled, making it easier to steer by skiing between the sled and the team, using the pole as a lever.

Despite the mushy trail and heavy sled we made good time. But five miles from home we hit the Old Channel, a slough notorious for spring flooding, which our unfortunate trail followed for several miles, crossing from one sandbar to the next.

The first couple of crossings proved safe enough. The river had flooded, with a foot and a half of water flowing on top of the solid winter ice, but the surface had already frozen. On the third bend the ice cracked as I walked softly across to check it. I gained the far side and called the dogs. They shot after me, the ice cracking in huge spiderwebs fifteen feet across all around Julie and the sled. If the dogs had slowed down the whole kit and caboodle would have fallen through.

I was on the gee pole at the next bend. The ice here looked safe, but fifteen feet from the far bank the leaders swerved and I saw a gaping hole dead ahead, open clear down to the running water below. My skis, tied into the towline, held me trapped as I skidded straight for that black hole, skittering sidewise across the rough overflow ice.

Julie abandoned the sled. She was helpless to stop it, and she had no intention of getting wet. At the last instant the big wheel dogs levered the sled to the side as they dodged the hole. One ski dipped precariously over the edge as I threw my weight against the pole. I felt the sled drop as the runner slid over the edge of the hole, but it righted itself again as we hit the sandbar.

I hopped awkwardly up the thawing mud bank and then glided easily as we hit snow. I told the dogs to whoa and waited for Julie and Jeff, my legs trembling. After that we never tied the skis to the towline; I just pulled myself along by holding the gee pole a little tighter. This not only proved safer, it allowed me to ski along, taking the load off the dogs.

Two more miles of treacherous river lay ahead, and I knew we'd be lucky to stay dry much longer. On the next bend I skied across easily ahead of the dogs, but the sled, with Julie driving, broke through halfway across and fell into the knee-deep water over the old ice. The dogs and sled plowed through the half-inch ice and water as Julie pushed from behind, slipping and sliding on the slick surface below the water. I grabbed the dripping lines as the leaders scrambled out, and helped them drag the sled ashore.

We had unloaded part of the gear before crossing in hopes of keeping the heavy sled from breaking through, and by the time Jeff and I ferried that gear across we were all soaked to the knees. Once safely ashore the three of us paused to consider our plight. The river grew progressively worse as we neared the mouth, with weaker ice and deeper flooding. Jeff's feet were cold from the freezing water, but Julie and I warmed right up. Twenty years of running barefoot to the outhouse down to sixty below finally paid off!

We decided to leave the river and cut through the thick willows to another old slough, which led us to where our trail left the Old Channel. Despite the deep, soft snow, dense willow patches and one dogfight, we eventually regained the regular route, safe if wet, with only a mile to go. Our first winter of trapping had come to a triumphant close.

Considering our vast supply of ignorance we didn't do badly; in two months we snagged thirteen marten, a fox, and two lynx, not to mention several beaver and a handful of muskrats taken in the spring. The total profit amounted to roughly one thousand dollars. We paid half that amount up front for the Birch Cabin and a short section of line Slim had sold to someone else before his death, and the other five hundred dollars barely covered our dog food bill.

Looking back, so many seemingly unendurable hardships would today be routine. With better dogs we can usually make the eighteen-mile run to the Birch Cabin in under two hours and it represents only a fraction of the line we regularly trap. To catch only thirteen marten in a season would mean living in a state of permanent bankruptcy, and we have never again had to resort to the use of the disintegrating Igloo Creek cabin because of bad trails. Knee-deep water is no cause for astonished fright, and extremes in weather we shrug off.

Yet for all that I think those few months were among the happiest of my life. Perhaps it was just the sharp contrast to our dreary winter life in town, or the fact that we had no requirements beyond living and loving it. We had lots of food, eight nice dogs and a warm cabin. It didn't matter whether we made money then, as we were still living off the money our folks put by for our college education.

Or maybe it was because we realized now without the slightest doubt what we wanted to do. We wanted to trap. We wanted to trap the way Slim had, by dog team, in the Shadow of Denali.

Again it was winter, our last as college students.

I scratched a hole through the quarter-inch of frost and

ice on the window and peered out at the thermometer. Forty below. Would it ever warm up?

Julie and I had returned home alone for the three-week Christmas break. We could not afford to fly the dogs out for that short a time, so we left them with Ray in Fairbanks, determined to go even if we walked everywhere. Our parents were off traveling again and we trudged the six miles from the airstrip across the snow-drifted lake, reaching home long after dark to a bitterly cold cabin. The cold was too intense to risk the eighteen-mile walk to the Birch Cabin. We lit a raging fire in the drum stove in Slim's cabin and huddled near it, fervently hoping for a break in the cold.

Every day we headed out on snowshoes, one of us traveling slowly, setting fox traps while the other pushed on out the trail, breaking it out as far as we could go and still make it home by late evening. Three days later the broken trail stretched halfway up, an eighteen-mile round trip.

One day when I was out wearing snowshoes and Julie was keeping the home fires burning, a rattle at the door caught her off guard. One does not expect company at forty below. She opened the door cautiously and saw the frosty figure of Ray Wildrick, Jr.

"We were wondering if you guys wanted to come over to my folks' place for Christmas potluck," Junior said, coming in and taking off his glasses to thaw them by the stove.

"Sure, I guess so," Julie said, "if it stays cold. We're going out when it warms up."

"I can come give you a ride over if you want," Ray offered, dark eyes anxious at the thought of our walking at forty below or maybe even lower.

"We can walk over," Julie replied, "but a ride back would be nice." A six-mile trek was a small price for the good food and good company that came hand in hand at Stella

Wildrick's Christmas get-togethers.

That evening we cooked up some fondant chocolate candies in anticipation of the party. But on Christmas eve we awoke to the sound of a howling wind ripping through the bare birch trees outside. Wind in the Interior means relief from the intense cold, as the gusts mix the cold surface air with warmer layers aloft. By afternoon the temperature warmed to a balmy fifteen below.

Julie and I made quick plans to head for the line cabin the next day. We had a small red plastic sled, the sort we'd played with as kids. We loaded it with eighty pounds of food, traps, bait, and cold-weather gear, and stuffed another forty pounds into a back pack. With just two and a half weeks left before we had to catch the mail plane back to school, we didn't intend to come back for more supplies. We would take the heavy load halfway, cache some, proceed with the rest, and have it all within reach of the trapping cabin.

Christmas Day, four-thirty a.m. Dressing warmly, we headed out into the wind-chill of sixty below. The gusts struck the hardest on the first half-mile stretch across open country, but the air snapped with life after the stifling cold, and the whirling wind filled us with euphoria.

Stars showed us the way, for the moon was gone and the sun would not lighten the sky for three hours. The major constellations lost their dominance in the billions of tinier stars around them, scattered like a brilliant haze beyond the pellucid atmosphere.

"*Merry Christmas!*" Julie yelled.

"*Merry Christmas!*" I roared, laughing into the wind. That's one nice thing about living in the bush — you can go out at five-thirty on Christmas morning and scream your heart out, and nobody except the wind will scream back.

With that heavy load we knew we had a bugger of a trip

ahead of us. I pulled the sled on skis, wearing a rope harness, while Julie went ahead with the pack. By the time daylight caught up with us, several miles already lay behind us.

Julie had cut away to check a side loop which rejoined the trail five miles out. When she caught me she triumphantly held up a fine mink, dark and fully prime, which she'd nabbed in a fox trap in a patch of cattails.

By the time we passed Igloo Creek cabin seven miles out, the rope harness cut bitterly into my shoulders and tiredness had set in. The skis merely kept me from sinking in the soft snowshoe trail — I couldn't slide while hauling that load. Julie, with the pack, fared a little better.

When we reached the end of my old snowshoe trail, Julie strapped on the snowshoes and trudged ahead, breaking out the trail. Luckily only six inches of snow lay in the open windblown areas, and not much more in the woods.

By the time we reached the point where we planned to cache the gear, I was about done in. But with the load cut in half my determination took a firm grip once more and we chugged on, slowly but steadily eating up one mile, another, and yet another, never stopping except for a quick bite of half-frozen lunch.

As darkness crept in Julie exchanged snowshoes for skis again and picked up her pace, anxious to set the trail over a difficult section before full darkness. I followed more slowly, still pacing myself, timing my energy right down to the very end.

When Julie hit the creek she slowed down. The last half-mile ran up the river, with its treacherous ice and open holes. In the blackness she couldn't see the ice to judge its safety.

Suddenly she heard the soft shuffling sounds of her skis change their tune, growing more resonant, echoing hollowly, and she froze. Was she skiing onto a patch of thin, hollow ice, with air beneath it and cold black water running swiftly below that? She hastily backtracked, and blocked the path with an X shaped from broken willows stuck in the snow so I would not follow those dead-end tracks. Only by the light of the following day did she see the hollow sound had not been made by the dreaded hollow ice, but by the peak of a hard-packed snowdrift.

I reached the cabin at six-thirty in total blackness, a few minutes behind Julie. I staggered into the chilly shelter as Julie huddled over the growing fire she had built in the stove.

"*Why* didn't we go to Stella's Christmas party?" I moaned, collapsing in a small heap on the bed. We'd been thirteen hours on the trail, with less than a half hour of rest during the entire day. Christmas dinner consisted of boiled rice with canned dried beef, and the most welcome gift was the twelve hours of solid rest on the cold pole bunks, interrupted only by the constant chore of fire-feeding.

Despite my weariness I snowshoed out a couple of miles the following day, while Julie rested up for the trip back for the supplies. As she headed out a day later, I snowshoed on again, but returned early to rest and cut wood.

At three in the afternoon I felt a sensation of change and I paused to listen. The wind had quit, and the first fingers of worry crept in. The cold would return fast and Julie only had ski boots to keep her feet warm. I hoped she'd beat it back.

She did. By five p.m. she came skiing in, breathless from maintaining a fast pace to keep warm. Dragging the little sled inside, she boomed, "Santa Claus is here again. He brings us food and cheer again!"

The temperature was twenty-seven below. By morning it had sunk to minus forty again.

Over the next four days the temperature hovered between forty and fifty below. We concentrated on setting out short lines, traveling on snowshoes. I worked my way out Slim's main trail, most of which I'd never been over before, and found it for a distance of about five miles, while Julie set traps on a couple of shorter loops. Once set up, we checked the traps every other day, but in the cold weather nothing was moving.

The cold broke just before New Year's Eve. A warm front brought the temperature up to zero, without the accompanying snow such weather often brings. We cut wood in our shirt-sleeves and icicles sprouted from the eaves of the roof.

On New Year's Day, one week after we had reached the Birch Cabin, Julie checked one line and I trekked out my five-mile trail. I returned with a bubbling heart. Julie was home already, sawing wood behind the cabin.

"How many did you get?" I called, confident that her luck had improved as well as mine with the coming of warm weather.

"Two!"

"Well, I guess five in two days isn't bad!" I sang.

"You caught *three*?" She sounded impressed.

"No, I caught *five*!" I whooped.

We celebrated New Year's Eve with a huge pot of dried beans, cooked with a precious can of ham. Oh, dear we ate a lot of those beans! Oh, we ate an *awful* lot of beans. They weren't quite done, but that didn't slow us down any.

In the wee hours of New Year's Day a loud crash jerked me from a dead sleep. Julie, on the top bunk, had leaped down and hit the floor running.

"What's wrong?" I demanded.

"I'm *sick*!" she exclaimed, banging out the door.

There followed a dreadful episode. Julie had a severe attack of what we call The Bean, or, more explicitly, a Severe Gastro-Intestinal Disorder. She was sick the rest of the night and a good bit of the following day.

I, on the other hand, weathered those beans with impunity and, laughing off Julie's foreboding admonitions, I devoured the leftovers for lunch.

I was sick for a week.

Beans or no, we celebrated New Year's Day by making a peach pie out of a can of carefully rationed fruit. With only four or five cans to last us the two weeks, this was truly a luxury of the highest degree, and a splendid concoction. I don't think we ate anything else, though.

In spite of the sickness we ran the short lines faithfully every other day, pulling in two or three marten each time. We were thrilled with our luck. Every few years marten seem to move in a great wave, migrating through an area and bringing riches to fortunate trappers. Whether this was happening or whether they were just hungry after the long cold, I don't know, but we sure did pull them in.

I'd found a spot where the otter slipped down a hole in the riverbank into the flowing water below the ice, and I set a trap there. Every time I headed out to check my marten line I looked hopefully at that set, only to be disappointed.

One afternoon, shortly after Julie had departed to run one of her lines, I was busy with the endless chore of chopping wood when I thought I heard her yelling.

"Yo!" I called.

"Yah!"

"What!"

"Yaaah!"

I figured either she had fallen into the river and was running home soaking wet, or she'd found something in my trap. I ran down the trail to meet her, and spied her holding a long, brown, sleek, slippery — otter!

I spent the rest of the afternoon skinning it out and scraping the fat off. Being aquatic animals, they're as bad as beaver for a fatty skin, but I didn't care. It was my first otter, and the first of anything is always a triumph.

I suppose being sick with The Bean drained me emotionally as well as physically. The hard work took its toll, and by our last evening at the trapping cabin I felt washed up despite the glow of success.

Julie and I sat down for a final dinner, and as usual started laughing about something. Without warning my laughter turned to tears, which rushed down my cheeks with alarming determination.

I sat mortified as Julie stared at me in surprise. This simply doesn't happen to me.

I leaped to my feet. "I think I'll go outside for awhile," I said brightly.

"Here," Julie offered quickly, to give me a good excuse. "Take the trash out."

Grateful for anything. I seized the cut-off gas can with its load of empty tins and fled into the darkness.

I stood outside by the corner of the little cabin, laughing and crying and wiping the tears away. In just a moment I regained my composure and reentered a more humble person. We finished the meal in total silence.

We pulled out early the following morning. We had caught seventeen marten in two weeks, better than we'd done in two months the previous winter. With our heavy parkas and fur mukluks packed away in the sled next to a burlap sack containing the precious furs, we headed for home, pulling traps as we went.

A couple miles from the end of Julie's last line I found another marten in a trap. That made eighteen. I called back to Julie, who had fallen behind as she picked up the traps, and she stopped to collect it while I pressed on. A short distance on I found our nineteenth marten. I called back, and she hurried along to get it.

She'd fallen way back by the time I approached the last set at the edge of a large lake. Would it give us an even twenty?

That was too much to ask for. But my heart was pounding as I drew near. Then I stopped, not believing our luck.

"Hallooo!" I yelled.

"Yo!" Julie's voice drifted back to me.

"Twenty!"

Twenty marten in two weeks of trapping. And we'd caught the first ones only a week ago.

The fox traps at the lower end were all blown in with snow, but we weren't complaining. Our most valuable Christmas present lay carefully wrapped in that big burlap bag.

Another few months of school loomed before us, big and black and boring. But then at last we'd be free, free from the obligation of getting an education, free from the long closed-in winters in town, free from the clutter and pressure of so many other people. We'd be free to be ourselves and pursue our dream.

# 4

# THE WAY OF LIFE

"**H**ere's the plan," Miki said through a mouthful of oatmeal, dried fruit and powdered whole milk. "We take six dogs to the Grayling Creek cabin. I'll ski on out Hilltop Trail, while you follow with the ax and brush it so we can get the dogs through there next time."

"Right," I said. We were eating breakfast at the small Spruce Cabin, forty-five miles from home. The cabin glowed with light from a Coleman lamp, but outside the winter morning light barely filtered through the snow-laden birch trees.

"At dusk you come home and I'll spend the night at Grayling Creek, go back over the hill early tomorrow, and come back here tomorrow night."

"OK," I said, glad I wasn't the one who would be staying in that tiny wilderness cabin Slim had built years ago.

Miki gulped the last of her breakfast and hopped up. "Here we go."

We hooked up the dogs and loaded the sled with trapping paraphernalia — bait, traps, ax, wire and Miki's overnight gear. Miki snapped on her skis and caught the towrope behind the six-foot wooden sled while I took the runners. The dogs, eager despite weeks of hard labor behind them, flew down the steep bank to the creek.

"Hey!"

The creek had overflowed during the night, and ten inches of blue water flowed through the snow. I urged Loki forward, but it was too deep for a safe crossing. We couldn't work all day with feet soaked to the knees.

"Come gee, Loki!" I called. Our big leader gladly swung the team back to the bank, where the deep, dry snow quickly absorbed the water from his black fur. A skim of ice had formed over the flooded creek a few yards upriver, and we crossed there.

"When you get home tonight, pack in enough water to last until we leave next week," Miki told me. "We won't have to melt snow and ice any more!"

"Right!"

"Oh, and light a fire at Grayling Creek when you leave tonight, and put my beans and cornbread on to thaw. I'll be getting in late tonight."

"Right."

"It would be nice if you cut some firewood there, too."

That'll take a bit of time, I thought, but cutting wood was easier than brushing trail, so I said, "OK."

We passed the first tepee-shaped marten cubby with the #1 longspring trap in its doorway. I didn't stop: I could bait the cubbies on the way home, after dropping off Miki. We bait the cubbies frequently to keep a fresh scent in the set, using whatever we have on hand — rotten moose guts, beaver castor, spoiled fish, grouse feathers and rabbit fur work well.

"What about the drags on the traps, what shape are they in?" I asked.

"Bad shape. Some are rotten and some are too small, and some aren't even wired onto the trap chains, they're just stuck in the loop." We had about eighteen sets along the six-mile trail, and replacing the drags which anchor the traps would be time-consuming, but we couldn't risk losing marten.

We crossed Windswept Ridge and a couple of lakes, climbed a hill and twisted above a torturously overgrown drainage, then plunged down the far side to land in a deep, narrow ditch, Grayling Creek. The sled jammed between two vertical banks which rose six feet apart, and I stepped forward to lift the bow of the sled up the bank. "Hike!"

Miki skied down the bank behind me and almost made it up the far side before she lost her balance. "Aa, aa!" she shrieked like a scared rabbit as she toppled over, to land upside-down in the ditch. "Aaa!"

"Stand up!" I shouted at her, laughing but chiding her, too. "I'm telling you, Miki, one of these days you're going to hurt yourself."

"I know," she said brightly, hazel eyes aglow with innocence.

The dogs winded a moose and loped the next mile while the sled bounced and flew over the muskeg. Keeping my feet on the jolting runners demanded a keen sense of balance, and more than once I slipped off and dragged, hands desperately clamped on the handlebow as I pulled myself upright.

"Stand up!" Miki roared with delight.

"Warn me before we reach the Horrible Hole," I called back.

"I think it's right up —"

Too late!

The dogs disappeared into the gully, struggling through brush, over massive tussocks and across waist-deep ditches. The sled crashed down the six-foot bank, rammed into a mammoth tussock, and slammed to a halt. I almost flew over the handlebow and an instant later Miki, skidding down behind the sled, slammed into me and knocked me breathless.

Gasping, I staggered forward to lift the sled over the tussock. One runner slid into a ditch and the sled flipped easily upside-down and wedged between two great frozen globs of grassy growth.

"I don't care what else you do, I want you to find a different spot to cross this creek!" Miki growled.

"It'll take two hours to cut a new trail through these alders," I protested. "You can walk across this creek on the trees and never touch the ground."

"I don't care, you'd jolly well better do it. I'd rather have a detour around this Horrible Hole than a mile of clear trail up the hill!"

I sighed. "You want me to clear out this patch, brush Hilltop, light the fire and start your supper, cut wood, bait all the cubbies, check all the drags *and* haul enough water to last us *and* the dogs four days."

"You can always build an outhouse behind Spruce Cabin if you run out of things to do," Miki suggested impishly.

"Sure, mac!" I picked up the sled. "Hike!"

The day's work had begun and a long day it was, though typical of most working days on the trapline. Most days find us on the trail, spending seven to ten hours driving dogs, brushing overgrown sections of trail, building new cubbies and maintaining old ones. Once or twice a week we take a day off to catch up on domestic chores — housework, pelt care and wood-cutting. It's a standing joke that we spend our precious days of rest cutting firewood with an ax and handsaw.

Because we trap seventy to ninety miles of trail each year, we frequently travel separately and spend many days alone on the trail, but loneliness is rarely a problem. Living alone for days or weeks lets you catch up on the thinking of deep thoughts, and things are more peaceful with nobody but your own conscience to tell you what to do, where to go, when to eat, sleep, read or work. It's different when you have a partner.

"Get up!" Miki shouts before the break of dawn. "Light the lantern!" she orders as I'm getting dressed. "Stir the oatmeal!" she says while I'm pumping the lantern.

"I'm lighting the lantern."

"Go give the dogs their morning snack!"

"I'm stirring the oatmeal."

"I'll do that, you go feed the dogs. And bring in some wood. And don't forget to turn those marten pelts."

"But I have to make my lunch, and —"

"Look out!" she warns. "I feel a bad mood coming on."

"You're already in a bad mood."

"A vicious mood! A temper tantrum!"

I laugh at her indignant expression. She glares angrily, but I keep snickering quietly under my breath until the tension breaks and she has to laugh, too.

Things are more peaceful when I'm alone. I become in tune with the silence around me. A constant alertness keeps me aware of every twig snap and fire crack. I feel I have not only the time but the obligation to pause and pay my respects to the stern beauty of the land.

At certain times the haunting, morose weight of loneliness does creep in. This usually happens right after Miki leaves for a few days out the line. After the sounds of jingling dog harnesses, creaking sled joints and spirited shouts die out, an oppressive silence fills the empty dog yard and cabin. I find myself alone, and lonely.

Not for long. Soon I'm singing as I haul wood, ski short trapping trails, or skin out fur. The lonesomeness fades, perhaps to return at dusk but only until the lantern's bright flare fills the cabin. For human companionship the radio mumbles constantly in the background, and if our parents are at home I contact them every couple of days on ham radio.

Again I feel lonely two hours before I expect Miki back. After blithely working for days without a word from her, I begin mulling over the countless problems she may have encountered — thin ice, overflow, moose, grizzlies, cabin fires, frozen feet, broken sled, broken leg or dogfights, and my heart chills.

Growing more and more depressed, I start stew and bannock for supper and cook up some concoction for dessert, such as berry pie, pudding, ice cream or a pound cake slow-baked in a fry-pan on the small stove top.

Finally I hear the jingle of towlines, the hissing of sled runners, and Miki's shout, tired but happy. I dash out to make sure, dart in to load up the fire, and rush excitedly back out. "How many marten?" I call.

"Thirteen!" A good haul. No matter how I enjoy being alone, it's pretty darn nice to have company again. We talk and talk. The dogs are icy and we let them all inside. They lie on the floor, on the beds, under the beds, under the table or by the stove. I pass around a pot of water; some drink and others look disgusted: they saw enough water on the trail.

The cabin is crowded and bursting with heat. The stove is loaded with good things to eat while ten gallons of dog food, cooked rice and fish and tallow, cool in buckets on the floor. Frozen fur animals and dog harnesses hang to thaw and Miki's gear is strewn across the floor between the stove, beds, table and woodpile. Around all this sit the ubiquitous five-gallon cans which seem to reproduce spontaneously in our cabins. I'm sitting in our Birch Cabin as I write this, and looking around I see five buckets of water and others full of dog rice, meat powder, tallow and commercial feed for the dogs, with one more for slop water, another for trash, and another for tanning animal skins. A couple of empty buckets are shoved under the bed.

When the temperature plunges to minus forty and colder we often stay off the trails, holing up and doing chores around the cabin. Although we can travel and have at fifty below, every risk is magnified, so we prefer to rest the dogs during these severe cold snaps, which usually last five to fifteen days.

"We've got four climate zones in here," I complained one day to Miki as we huddled over the stove. "The tropical zone goes a few inches away from the stove and the temperate zone reaches my top bunk, but the table is definitely in the Arctic zone, and so are the potatoes — I moved them right next to the fire, but they're still freezing. We have to get them off the floor."

"And my bed is in the polar zone," Miki added morosely. "I think I froze my nose last night, even with the roaring fire."

This is the time to make ice cream. I stir whole powdered milk in water to make a smooth mixture and add sugar (too much) and vanilla ('way too much) and pour this into a clean topless one-gallon Blazo can. Outside, the milk freezes quickly because we never make ice cream when it's warmer than minus ten. The mixture would freeze so slowly we'd forget to stir it, producing "ice" instead of "cream."

As the mixture thickens, we have to stir it often to break up the crystals. Bringing it inside, we shove the pan under the table in a ten-below draft so we can stir it without running outside in the snapping cold air.

Wearing mukluks at dinner, we wolf down moose ribs, garden broccoli and potatoes from last summer's harvest, and pilot-bread crackers. Then Miki stirs up a rich hot chocolate sauce. Out comes the ice cream from under the table; we put so much hot sauce on, it's all melted before we can eat it, and we wonder why we bothered to freeze it at all.

During one particularly long fifty-below spell we were cramped in a cabin with only candles for light, and a tiny radio that rarely worked to link us occasionally with the outside world. One evening I began fiddling with the radio dial, trying to make it work, and for just a few seconds a weather forecast came in from Fairbanks.

"And for tomorrow, temperatures ranging to twenty above. . ."

"*Above?* Did he say twenty *above?* He must have got it wrong!" I frantically wiggled the dial, but the radio was dead.

The next day it was twenty above. We hurried eagerly back to work, glad our enforced vacation was over.

And work it is, too. We run the trails once a week to maintain sets and bring in the fur, and we also have a great deal of trail work to do because the line is so old. Each year we pick an old trail we have never traveled and work our way out the line, finding old blazes, clearing the trail, repairing old cubbies or building new ones. Forty years may have passed since the trail was last used, and it may be so overgrown it's unrecognizable except for an occasional blaze. Each time it angles up a creek, pothole or lake we anticipate spending hours searching for the trail on the far side, and sometimes an old scar made by a sled runner hitting a tree is the only clue that a trail once passed here.

Some of the creeks are chock full of dwarf birch, alder and willows that must be cleared. Once I had to follow an old trail which had been overgrown, burned by a forest fire, and overgrown again by young trees and shrubs sprouting among the blackened stumps. As we forge into new country we come across creeks, lakes and hills which we often name, not from egotism but to make communication easier:

"Where'd you get that big black marten?" Miki might

ask when I come in with a fresh catch.

"You know the slough after the Old Channel, and the wolf set and a couple other sets, and then we cross the creek where we found those big snails that summer, you know? And then we go through the sort of tunnel in the willows. He was in those willows."

So much easier to say, "In Willow Alley near Clear Creek."

Thus many of our landmarks have names like Three Corners, Caribou Corner, Fox Fork, Otter Bank, the Notch, the Bush and Windswept Ridge. Many lakes, boggy little ponds mostly, are named too: Rat Lake, Sunset Lake, Beaver Puddle, Wolverine Lake, Beaver-Dot Lakes One, Two, and Three, Straight-Across Lake and Way-the-heck-and-gone Lake.

For some reason creeks always give us trouble. Many are deep ditches, twisting and filled with tussocks and stumps and brush. We often lose Slim's overgrown trails here, and many hours go into finding and clearing the trails at these crossings. This reflects in our naming of the creeks: Frustration Creek, Too-Deep Creek, Smash-it-up Creek, Give-it-up Creek, Horrible Hole and Dreadful Ditch. Only a few have prettier names like Whisper Creek and Otter Slough.

The Haunted Forest is a queer place, hardly thirty feet wide as it stretches across the trail, but dark and gloomy, repelling the light cast on either side of the gray timber. Old spruce keep mysteriously falling to block the trail. Beneath my feet, the ground rumbles sickeningly and suddenly collapses: shell ice, over three feet of air, a hidden drainage treacherously cluttered with tangled logs. Within the Haunted Forest, a small marten cubby.

"Pitch black," I told Miki. "Thick overcast night and the dogs started running like crazy when we came near the Haunted Forest. I didn't think anything was in the set since I'd passed it that morning, but I had to make sure. It was so dark I couldn't see anything, so I bent down to peer inside the cubby, and I heard this frightful scream in my ear. A marten was sitting on *top* of the cubby. He almost got my nose! I was scared!"

For all the work involved in finding and clearing old trails, we still count ourselves lucky to have a trapline at all. Despite the width and breadth of Alaska, very little land is available to new trappers. If it's not in use now, it's probably starvation country.

With the prime land taken, it's hard to obtain a trapline today. You can grow up in a trapping family or inherit the line, as we did. Sometimes you can buy a trapline, or go partners with a trapper. But simply cutting a trail where he pleases may lead a person into a violent confrontation if an established trapper's area is trespassed. Trappers take their work very seriously, and a threat against one's livelihood can turn a mild man vicious.

This is partly because in Alaska a trapper does not legally own his trapline, nor even his cabins unless he's lucky enough to own a parcel of land under each cabin. Canada has laws to protect a trapper's rights but Alaska does not, so while Alaskans have fewer restrictions, they also have to protect their own turf.

Miki and I trap an area of about 800 square miles, bounded by five other traplines. We have an understanding with our neighbors about the boundaries and we trust these men — Leonard and Tom, Paul and Gary and Jack. We know they will not break their word any more than we would break ours.

Some trappers rely on their furs as their main source of income; they need that fur money to survive. Others trap to supplement bank accounts founded on more stable sources of income. Miki and I fall halfway between the two. Trapping provides most of our income, outstripping our freelance writing and sales of handcrafts, but thanks to careful investments

Daddy has made over the last thirty years, our fur money is not critical to our survival. Should the fur markets fail or the land dry up, we have something to fall back on.

Each trapper has his preferred method of travel. Some ski or snowshoe or hike, but the stretches of land covered by professional trappers require a faster way. Most trappers use snow machines, but Miki and I have always used dogs. We run dogs because fixing snow machines is not in our repertoire of skills, because I can't endure the noise of those machines, and because we enjoy working with dogs. Slim traveled exclusively by dog team or on foot, and I am proud to see our dogs' feet fall on the same trails as did the big feet of his old huskies.

The airplane has played a part in this area ever since the first mail flight in 1924. For decades Slim asked a bush pilot, frequently Daddy, to fly a thousand fish to his trapline each winter. Although Miki and I both fly, we are ground-lovers in the winter. Still, Daddy or our brother Ray often gets out once or twice a year with a load of dog feed for us. I don't do enough winter flying to feel competent to land a ski plane on a tiny lake out there, much less cope with complications such as overflow or an engine too cold to start. We do fly out on the trapline during the summer, though, to do summer repairs, pick berries and build dog houses (we *always* need one more dog house). The only landing spots are four to six miles from the cabins, and the trek in involves crossing glacial rivers and creeks, but it's well worth the effort for the happy times we have there.

Considering the number of miles we travel in all kinds of weather, we're lucky to have so far escaped serious injuries on the trapline. Still, accidents do happen frequently and we must be prepared to cope with the unexpected by carrying matches, extra clothing, repair materials and a first-aid kit.

Most accidents are minor and generally involve crashing. The dogsled crashes into trees, banks and stumps. When skijoring behind sled dogs, you can crash into any of these things or crash for no reason at all.

"The dogs were pretty wild today," I'll tell Miki. "The sled climbed a few trees, knocked some down and, um, I sort of broke the headboard and a few basket slats and the towrope and one stanchion." Although the shaped and lashed white ash strips that make our sleds are supple and strong, a rough trail and a powerful team can wreak havoc on them. Broken boards must be splinted or replaced, and repairing sleds has delayed my bedtime on many a weary night.

Most crashes result in bruised knees and shins, but they can be more serious. While zipping down a mountainside in Denali Park once, Miki crashed into Wonder Lake and had a shocking black eye for a few days. She's also gotten some bad bruises on her knees while skijoring — large, impressive bruises, the kind that bounce when you walk. Twice I've knocked myself out by careening into trees, and I also have a tendency toward breaking teeth.

Cuts made while skinning, burns from the stove and sore muscles from strenuous work are all matter of course. Most of these are left to get well on their own.

When I'm traveling alone, I'm more careful to avoid situations where I might get into serious trouble. I think twice before swinging an ax haphazardly, or skiing down a steep bank, or crossing hollow ice. Catching a hand in a trap sometimes happens, but though annoying it's rarely dangerous. Larger traps can be difficult to open and painful, however, so extra care is required when working with wolf and wolverine traps.

Miki once set a trap for otters and mink in a small bank hole leading to the water under the lake ice. She set the trap, but as she lowered it down to a shelf just above the water, she accidentally sprung it on her hand. When she tried to pull her hand out, the trap wedged in the hole. She was stuck.

She crouched there for several minutes, twisting and turning and writhing, but she couldn't get the trap out and she couldn't fit her free hand into the hole to release her fingers. At last she got scared and just yanked her hand out, to the detriment of a few fingernails and her glove. Had the trap been a little bigger she might still be there, a permanent monument to the trapper's risks.

I never know what might happen when I hit the trail each day. Usually nothing happens, but things can get interesting in a hurry. One day I headed out on skis with old Trapper, a malemute who had been retired from the team but who still made a good companion and pack dog. Trap was good about keeping away from animals in traps, but this day he forgot himself when we came upon a small marten caught in my best cubby.

"Trap! Stay back!" I roared, but too late. He charged past me to attack the small animal and the fight was over in an instant. As the eighty-pound husky closed in for the kill, the little marten shot up, grabbed Trapper by the nose, and threw him to the ground.

Well, maybe Trap fell to the ground, but by the time I took another breath he was on his belly screaming for mercy as the three-pound dead weight clung to his nose. Trapper could have killed the marten if he had thought to, but he was hurting too much. He was always afraid of pain. Except when he got crazy in a dogfight, he just wasn't a brave dog. Chivalrous and gallant in a good-natured sort of way, maybe, but not brave. I finally took pity on the blubbering knight and rescued him.

"There, you old dog! Maybe I won't bring you next time, for all you're worth!" But I did bring him, of course, and a good thing.

This same cubby, set in birch by the river, had caught one marten after another for three weeks, but the next time I returned it held a small lynx. Still alive, he crouched motionless, staring at me.

"You stay back, Trap," I ordered. Those long claws and sharp teeth could really hurt a dog if he forgot himself. I was carrying an ax instead of a rifle, as I had been brushing trail, and I got lazy. Instead of cutting a long pole so I could reach the lynx from a distance, I edged in close and swung my ax, intending to knock him out. Before I could hit the lynx he attacked me.

The trap held one paw firmly, but his long, supple body easily reached me. Before I could leap back his powerful claws sank into my calf, pinning my leg as his jaws clamped onto my ankle , jerked and tore, and clamped down again.

I jumped back and he tripped me, throwing me floundering in deep snow. With my ankle snagged between his claws and teeth, I couldn't escape.

Trapper held back until I was attacked, and then hurtled into the fray. The lynx sprang at Trapper just as the dog snapped at him. Trapper missed; the cat did not. He gave Trap two solid bites before the old dog wrested free and fled screaming down the trail.

Trapper gave me the heartbeat of time needed to make my escape. I staggered back all a-tremble, quickly cut a green tamarack pole, and killed the lynx from a safe distance. Trapper was hiding in the trees. He came reluctantly when I called him and gave him a shaky hug. "Good boy," I said. We went on down the trail despite the burning in my leg, and picked up the lynx on the way back.

Trapper wasn't hurt so much as he let on, but later when I peeled off my thick wool socks, I found some deep bruises and a couple of punctures in my leg. One hole was the size of the cat's eyetooth, a half-inch deep and a quarter-inch around. I cleaned the wounds and dosed them with Cut-Heal, a horse liniment we use on our dogs' feet. It contains turpentine and sulfuric acid, which I figured would do the trick. I packed the worst hole with Furacin powder, another excellent vet product, and the puncture healed with a splendid scar. And we fed our dogs for a month with the money from the lynx pelt.

Although we kill the animals we trap as quickly and humanely as possible, sometimes things do go wrong and the creature suffers unduly. Yet by the law of the wild, most animals will die a gruesome death by starvation, lingering injury or murder by other hungry animals.

Furthermore, demand for pelts will be met, if not by trappers, then by fur-farmers who keep their animals caged. A wild animal, born to roam freely, probably would prefer a free life and a horrible death to being caged and then clubbed or gassed or electrocuted after a short maturation. And of course no serious trapper will let the animal populations fall below safe levels in his trapping area.

Trapline life has many inconveniences, from lack of modern facilities like indoor plumbing and electricity to living with the cold and dark, but they can be annoying or amusing, depending upon how you cope with them. For instance, to get water we must cut a hole through two or three feet of river ice, or melt snow or ice. Flat-tasting snow-water is full of birch seeds and spruce needles and takes plenty of firewood to melt, but lake water has its hazards as well.

Once Miki poured lake water from a pitcher into her bowl of powdered milk for her cereal, and as she stirred it she caught her breath and stared at the frothy milk.

"A leech!" she shouted. "A leech in my milk! Sick! Icky-ick!"

I roared with laughter as she scooped out a tablespoon of milk with the leech squirming indignantly and dumped it into the dog bucket. Still, I checked my own bowl of milk mighty carefully before pouring in my bran flakes.

Another time Miki was mixing a glass of instant drink when she gave a snort and dumped the whole glassful into the slop bucket. "I don't mind leeches," she complained, "but I won't drink fleas in my Tang! He probably had tapeworm eggs all through him. I told you not to hang those marten so close to the water buckets."

Fleas from the animals we catch aren't the only pests we live with. Mice hide beans and rice in our boots and drown themselves in our water buckets, while shrews sometimes eat tunnels through loaves of bread. Outside, ravens, jays, squirrels and marten will steal any meat, fish or dog food left exposed, and if a wolverine comes into camp he can really make trouble.

Visits from larger animals usually come most unexpectedly, such as the time I was skiing a short spur, carrying nothing but a bait can of rotten fish. I noticed a fox trap had been sprung, and moving closer I saw grizzly tracks. In the December dusk I stared at those big tracks leading into the brush, and then glanced uneasily at my volatile can of fish. Then I fled, keeping an eye to the rear and never mind the rest of my trapline. For the next month I carried a pistol while skiing and a rifle in the dogsled.

The thing about trapping is that you have to love it or you couldn't stand it. When you finally get your trails broken out, a big snow falls and again you must break out every mile of trail and clean out every one of one hundred and fifty or so sets. Then a freezing rain falls and the ice-covered traps are incapacitated until you break every one loose again.

Coming home at day's end often means arriving after sunset at a small, dark cabin as cold inside as out. The dogs must be unhitched and picketed, the fire lit, gear packed in, and water fetched or snow started melting. Frozen marten must be hung up to thaw, frozen fish chopped up and cooked for the dogs. After supper we have animals to skin, the dogs to feed, and perhaps some repair work or wood-cutting to complete before the aching body can be laid to rest on a spruce-pole bunk.

Even a small mishap along the trail, a broken sled or an animal torn loose which must be tracked down, can cause great delays. One day the clamp of my ski binding broke and with no wire or string, I couldn't jury-rig a repair. I hopped along for three miles on one ski, feeling ridiculous as I carried the broken ski in one hand and the rifle in the other. With two marten, a burlap sack and a pair of frozen gloves bulging in my coat pockets, I slid awkwardly along, grumbling quietly to myself, but still I laughed when I recalled Miki's silly parody of an old nursery jingle:

"Deedle deedle dumpling, my son John! Went to bed with his ski boots on — one ski off and one ski on, deedle deedle dumpling, my son John!"

And yet there are rewards for this life we lead. Bales of fine, well-finished pelts mean money in the bank and dog food in the shed. Other rewards mean more even if they are less critical to survival.

It's exciting to travel through the long dark of December. When the sun peeps over the mountains at eleven-thirty in the morning, I shout to the dogs, "Sun's up! Better get a move on, it'll be dark soon!"

I don't miss the long days of summer. Then again, when the sun does return, the bright blue skies and beautiful, wind-tossed sunbeams shed joy over all the land. I want to throw back my parka hood, dash off my fur hat, and turn my face toward the precious golden warmth.

But it's queer how beautiful the light is when the December sun lies low on the horizon. Summer colors of blue and green seem harsh compared to the softer grays and blues of midwinter. Traveling at sunrise, with the sky shedding a soft blue-gray or pink light over spruce heavily laden with snow, I have the sensation of moving through the pastel colors of a three-dimensional painting. At dusk, one feels enveloped in the breathtaking Arctic blue of approaching night, while frosty white tamarack limbs hang motionless in the still, silent air.

After sunset, when the moon is so bright you can see the shadow of your breath, traveling can bring out all the elation a body can know, with the white-winged trees flying past eagerly bounding dogs. Or in the dark of the moon, when nothing can be seen at all, you are submerged in the sounds of your skis gliding over drifted snow, crusty ice, soft snow and then frosty ice, while the strong dogs pulling you patter swiftly down the trail.

Above the scenes of silver moonlight or blue dusk or pastel dawn, Denali rises in silent majesty, the dominant feature of all the land, its North Face somber in the midwinter dusk, or glowing white and blue and gray as the March sun swings north. Viewed from the highest point of our trapline, twenty miles from Denali's base, the sunlit granite and snow faces knock me breathless every time.

Because I love the land so, I see beauty even on the gloomy days. Whether going out on a brilliant, blustery March afternoon or a frosty, foggy December morning, I can't help looking wide-eyed around me and crying out to the dogs, "What a lovely, lovely day!"

Late one clear, windy, moonless night, I slipped from my wall tent to take a last look before turning in. The dogs, content after their evening meal, lay curled against the crispy ten-below wind. A feeling of wild joy and gratefulness filled my soul, but I whispered quietly lest some evil spirit hear me — more a thought than a whisper — "This is just as it should be, just the wind and the stars and the dogs and me."

# 5

# TRAPLINE TRAVELER

The anticipation of catching a big animal like a lynx or wolverine can bring thrills and chills when we see fresh tracks headed straight for a set. Will the animal truck right on by — the usual case — or will hunger or curiosity lead it to investigate the scent of rotted fish near the concealed trap?

One day my dogs winded a fresh scent, and as they picked up their gait I whooped them on, glad for the chance to ride the runners instead of pedaling and walking through the deep, new-fallen snow. With only six dogs the going had been painfully slow, but the scent put the spark back into the dogs and they remembered long-forgotten reserves of energy.

We flashed past a set of tracks across the trail, fresh and large, too big for fox or marten and not right for a wolverine. A lynx or wolf, I thought, but the loose, deep snow had sloughed into the prints and I couldn't tell which.

Julie had cached some dried fish a short distance ahead, setting a big No. $3^1/_2$ jump trap to protect the food from marauding animals and (we hoped) catch a marten or wolverine. It was still half a mile away, and I didn't have much hope the animal would pass that way.

But again I saw the tracks, crisscrossing the dogsled trail, and then again. He smells that fish, I thought. He's tracking it down, zigzagging into the wind to follow the scent. He must be hungry to go after it so determinedly. Must be a lynx. The tracks just weren't right for a wolf, although they were the same size. With his big feet and light build, a lynx usually floats across the surface of the snow, but here in the trees the powder lay deep and soft, so he sank in as the wolves do.

The dogs slowed, panting heavily. When Loki crossed the tracks again he charged forward and the rest of the team hurtled after the leader. Ivanhoe, bright and conceited, ran just behind Loki, followed by Mitsy and Rusty, and then the two big wheel dogs, Comet and Streak, still just pups.

The bank of the creek lay just ahead. The dogs hit top speed as they reached the steep twenty-foot incline leading down through the willows. When Loki hit the ice his ears shot forward and I knew I had something in that set.

Julie had put the fish on a bushy hummock protruding into the river and set the trap at its base, in a narrow aisle leading through the willows. A small stick propped at an angle just in front of the trap encouraged the animal to step over it onto the trigger of the trap, which lay in a slight hollow, disguised under white tissue and a sprinkling of snow.

Loki never stopped. He tore around the curve, the team barreling after him. I jumped on the sled brake, bearing down for all I was worth, but they didn't even feel the drag. As I swooped down onto the creek and whipped around the right-angle turn at the bottom, I saw the lynx.

He was huge, tawny-gray, the black-tufted ears laid back flat against the short, broad head, thin black lips drawn up in a silent snarl. The golden-green eyes held as baleful a glare as any cat could ever muster.

The dogs didn't hesitate. Loki darted straight at the big cat, tackling it in his fearless, calculating way.

The lynx was caught by three toes of one front foot and he'd been there just long enough to get hopping mad. His other front paw was armed with four very long, very sharp claws, and he was ready to fight.

As Loki grabbed him the lynx slashed at the big husky, spiking his shoulder. Loki leaped aside just as Ivanhoe closed in. Loki snarled at him, and the younger dog hesitated as Loki darted in at the trapped animal again. The lynx whirled toward him and the dog stopped, tense and quivering, caution reining in his instinct to kill.

The other dogs pressed forward more warily, the pups excited and leaping in their harnesses but afraid to approach the snarling lynx. I left the runners, whip in hand, and caught the towline to drag the dogs away. That whip told them I was serious, and I didn't even have to pop it to pull their attention from the lynx. Loki was still snarling softly to himself, but he followed me back to the trail and held the dogs there while I quickly killed the lynx.

Holding the cat up with the front paws above my head, I could barely get the hind feet off the ground. The big snowshoe feet looked deceptively soft, hiding half-inch sheathed claws. A big lynx was worth two or three hundred dollars and I yelped ecstatically.

I met Julie on the trail home, where I'd dropped her off earlier to brush the trail. The dogs winded her two bends away and began to run. I let them pass her before stopping.

"There was a really big lynx out the line," I said, holding back a twisted smile. "I was just sure I was going to get him."

"Oh, yeah?" Her eyes glowed.

"Yeah." I paused, and then flipped back the sled tarp to reveal the payment of the next month's dog food bills.

"Oh, my goodness!"

I grinned. We'd caught lynx before, but never this big. Our brother once caught one which stretched more than sixty inches from nose to tail, and while this lynx couldn't beat that, it was nothing to sneeze at.

Killing an animal in a trap is unpleasant. We do it as swiftly and humanely as possible: a quick blow to knock the animal senseless and then pinch the chest to stop the heart. Some larger animals are best shot; wolverine can be especially nasty. The first one we caught was in a small fox trap, and even though the trap was wired and chained to the drag, the wolverine got it off the spruce pole with its furious bearlike power. Julie lit out after it when she saw the telltale drag marks ending with tracks taking off down the edge of a lake. Because of grizzly sign in the area she was carrying a .308 — too large for shooting small game but better than nothing.

After she had floundered through the deep snow for an hour, Julie paused. The tracks simply disappeared into the drifts — the animal had gone to ground, tunneling under the snow. Cautiously she circled the spot, climbing onto a snowdrift to look for an exit hole. She didn't see any. But from right beneath her feet came the soft rustling of shifting snow under the hard-packed drift.

Julie shot straight up and landed about six feet away, rifle raised and ready. An instant later the wolverine erupted from the snowdrift. She didn't wait to see whether it was ready to attack — a quick shot in the heart finished the job. She was lucky to have found the animal, for they can travel for miles even dragging a trap, but she was just as relieved to have been out of reach when it surfaced.

Trapping is always a challenge and a gamble. Day after day we go out in all weather, never knowing whether we'll come back tired and loaded with five hundred dollars worth of furs, or just tired. Often we trudge along for days without bringing in a dime, but once we caught three lynx in ten days, when they were going for four hundred dollars each.

But fur animals are not the only creatures we are concerned with. Moose and bears can pose hazards at any time. I've never actually seen a winter bear except for the one the dogs chased in Denali, but I've seen their tracks in every month of the year. One January I came across the big, shuffling sign of a grizzly as he plodded up the river less than a mile from our home. Since we rarely carry a heavy rifle, meeting up with one of these well-armed animals could prove extremely dangerous, especially as our dogs seem sadly lacking in the fear and respect these big bears demand on a lean winter day.

We frequently run into moose, but around here they are wary and rarely cause problems. Excited though the dogs might be, they usually stick to the trail while the moose high-steps it away. Of course, when the moose is IN the trail, the situation is different.

When I ran into an old fellow just a mile from home, he stood resolutely on the hard-packed trail, unwilling to step off into the deep snow on the sides. Nor, apparently, did he have any reason for heading on down the trail. He just stood frowning balefully at me as I struggled to stop my dogs. Their maniacal desire to slaughter the fifteen-hundred-pound animal likewise did not impress him. I managed to stop the team about a hundred feet before the end of the world, holding it back with the sled brake while that old moose rolled his eyes, glaring at this bothersome interruption.

"Gi'-root-a here, ya bloody bugger!" I roared.

The moose stood firm, but the dogs took my words as encouragement and with a unified heave-ho they inched another few feet toward the moose.

"Whoo-aa," I growled.

The moose swung his head suspiciously. The dogs paused, then hit their harnesses again.

I had a .44 pistol but didn't want to use it. Instead I pulled out a short whip and popped it loudly. Although I rarely have to use it on the dogs, they know when I pop that whip I am not bluffing. They faltered at the sound, and apparently the moose also had respect for it, for he stepped off the trail and swung on his way in great long strides, allowing us to pass.

Actually, run-ins with animals are usually the least of our problems. Weather accounts for more hardship and hold-ups than everything else combined. Too much snow means breaking out eighty miles of trail on snowshoes, traveling at one or two miles an hour. Too little snow means banging over foot-high tussocks with the sled tossing and jerking, tipping over at every chance. Warmth actually causes more problems than cold. With a warm spell the creeks overflow, the swamp ice turns soft, and traps sink into wet snow and freeze. Although forty below is more common than forty above, rain can come even in the darkest days of December and January.

We were setting a new trail up the creek during one such warm spell. Julie had the team and sled loaded with traps and bait, while I skijored ahead breaking trail. A light drizzle filtered down through a dreary December sky.

"Oh dear, it's ra-aining again!" I sang. "I can't believe it's thirty-seven above! More than seventy degrees warmer than three days ago."

The hot wind had come barreling in from the south-west, bringing heavy snow and now this rain. An inch of water had accumulated on the ice under eight inches of snow, but the dogs marched right through it, pulling hard. We traveled only four or five miles an hour breaking trail, and the wind drove the rain into my shirt until I had to zip up my jacket despite the sweat from the hard work congealing on my back.

Julie had a ski trail winding through the trees that paralleled the creek for eight miles. We planned to reach the end of that, setting along the river instead so we could run the dogs up it.

"I marked the end out on the river with a spruce tree," she said when we stopped to let the panting dogs cool off. Water drained down Legs' white coat as he plopped into the slush.

"Is that a dead rat on your head?" Julie asked, scrutinizing my soggy marten hat.

"Yours looks just as bad," I laughed. The water matted the soft fur so her warm hat looked like a very dead rat kill.

We pushed on, passing some open water and an eagle's nest, tracing the tracks of nine caribou as they meandered upriver. I stopped after a couple more miles. The dogs were getting hot and tired, and I was dragging awfully hard. In the deep, sticky snow I couldn't help them by skiing along as I usually did.

Julie caught up, her dogs hot and panting.

"And all the time the rain came down in a most unpleasant way, Sir!" she sang in a sepulchral voice in a melodramatic minor key.

With all that water I was glad I had Loki in the lead. Although age was slowing the powerful husky, he'd still skirt dangerous spots or march straight through any water when I gave him the command. In places the dogs were splashing through five inches of overflow, but Loki kept gamely on.

Somehow we missed Julie's marker and trekked several miles too far. Except for some otter tracks and caribou sign, we saw no fresh tracks until we were about to turn back. There a set of lynx tracks tiptoed up the side of the river, water showing in the bottom of each one. I made a quick set, tying a beaver tail to a willow tree and hiding the trap in a trail stomped in the snow below.

"Hope the water doesn't come up and freeze that in," Julie said, critically surveying my work.

"It's raining, it's pouring, the o-old man is snoring," I chortled.

(Julie's prediction came true. When I returned later I found six inches of ice and eight inches of water over the trap.)

The rain fell steadily as we headed home through an early dusk. Julie finally spied her marker, a little spruce tree dripping sadly in the middle of the river, cleverly disguised in a coat of heavy, wet snow.

"Good run, about twenty-four miles, I think," Julie said as we unharnessed the icy dogs in the dark outside the cabin.

And all the time the rain came down in a most unpleasant way, Sir!

Warm weather isn't necessary to create water problems. The upper part of our creek is notorious for overflowing and glaciering with layers of ice. Although our dogs usually march right through water, it frequently causes serious problems. Slush sticks to the sled runners, dogs and gear get wet, and feet may freeze. Water is bad enough when one is wearing boots or mukluks, downright dangerous when it soaks ankle-high ski boots not known for their warmth in the first place. We always carry a change of footgear when traveling this creek, which has proved wise more than once.

I was on the home stretch to Spruce Cabin late one afternoon, looking forward to dinner and a good rest after breaking out twenty-seven miles of trail through a fresh snow-fall. To ease the load on my six dogs, I'd tied a gee pole onto the sled and skied ahead of it, steering with the pole to keep my weight off the runners.

As we came around a bend I suddenly sensed something was wrong. The dogs lost their power, then just stopped pulling. Loki glanced back as the sled coasted to a stop. But only when I began sinking did I realize what was wrong.

Overflow. The water had come up six inches under the deep, powdery snow, invisibly flooding the creek ice under the drifts. It lay hidden beneath the crust of the trail, but under our weight the dampened snow gave way and the dogs fell through. As they stopped my skis sank into the slush and frigid snow-water gushed into the low ski boots. Clutching the gee pole, I felt it twist as the heavily loaded sled broke through behind me.

At zero degrees the freezing slush locked in around the runners, stanchions, and even up around the high sled basket. I drove my hand into the watery snow and unclipped my skis. The snowshoes lay under the sled load and I jerked them out.

The dogs stood inches deep in the slush, watching anxiously as I snowshoed up to a sandbar. Hurrying down the strip of land, I dropped back to the trail. Even here I found water, but not too much. By now wet snow packed my boots and my feet were stinging something fierce. As I rushed back to the team I knew my feet would start freezing in a matter of minutes.

"Gee, Loki!" I cried as I came abreast of the big leader. "Gee! *Hike!*"

He knew what I wanted. Swinging to the right, he plunged into chest-deep snow, struggling to reach my broken trail, dragging the floundering team behind him. As he passed me I seized the towline and, gasping as needles of cold shot through my feet, I dragged the team onto the bank until they cleared the water.

I almost stopped then to change footgear, but as I reached the sled I saw with alarm how fast it was freezing in. The slush, exposed to the cold air, set up and froze all around it. Grabbing the bush bow, I gave the sled a wrench. At first it hardly moved, but as I heaved again the slush fell away. In one-step stages I dragged it out of the water and then sat down, jerking open the canvas tarp enclosing the load to pull out my mukluks and extra socks. I was tempted to put on my boots in case I hit more water; the soft leather mukluk soles weren't reliably waterproof. But I doubted my feet could warm up in the cold, stiff, rubber-soled leather boots.

I tore off my ski boots. They fell from my hands like heavy chunks of ice and clumped as I dropped them into the sled. When I peeled off the half-frozen socks to look anxiously at my feet, I saw the ugly yellow-white warning signs of frostbite across the soles, but, clutching each one in my hands, I felt they were not frozen beyond the outer layer of calloused skin. The moment I pulled on dry wool socks and fur mukluks the warmth flooded into them.

My feet safe, I turned my attention to the dogs. The deep, dry snow absorbed the water from their fur and they lay licking their feet vigorously. I tipped the sled over and banged the ice off with the back of the ax-head and then, setting it right, I cried, "Hike!"

Loki drove forward and the other dogs followed his lead. The sled crept ahead slowly, plowing in the soft snow, but Loki kept the team moving until we regained the trail. The light had slipped away and I was sure glad the cabin lay only a mile or two away. We'd be there before full darkness, I figured, although the deepening gloom cast an ominous feeling over the narrow creek.

Two more bends and we hit water again. I tried to keep the dogs moving, but once the sled broke through I knew we'd had it. The overflow here was starting to freeze. While the crust supported some weight, once we fell in the team would not be able to pull the sled through it. The moment I stepped off the runners to push I also fell into the six inches of slushy water.

"Hike!" I ordered sharply. Loki jerked forward with a power that brought the other dogs quickly into action. No good. They banged that towline tight, but the sled didn't budge.

I climbed onto the load. The water hadn't yet seeped into my mukluks, old though they were, and I didn't want to stand in the slush. I set a snowshoe down and stepped on it, heaved up the bush bow, and set the front of the sled up on the frozen crust.

"Hike!" I roared.

This time the dogs pulled the sled forward as I lifted the front clear of the ice. But I couldn't ride without having it sink in, and I couldn't walk without falling through. I tried snowshoeing behind the sled, but I couldn't jog with the snowshoes loaded with slush that froze to the ice with every step. After three heroic leaps I tripped up. The dogs kept on for a few yards, until the sled slid off the hardened trail into the soft powder and sank through the water under the snow.

I spent half an hour trying to cover fifty feet. As the sled grew heavier with freezing ice it demanded increasing strength to lift it onto the firmer trail. I strained again and again until, with a desperate tearing wrench, I'd drag it to the top of the crust. The dogs would haul it forward a few feet until it either ran off the trail or broke through again.

"Oh, man," I whispered, hunching over the load. "Oh, man." I felt all crippled up from the straining. I glanced over at the dogs. Loki was looking back, waiting. I never would have made it that far without him. He knew not to waste his efforts when the sled jammed, but when I gave the word he drove the team forward with powerful determination.

"Good boys," I said, a tremble creeping into my voice. "It'll be OK. We'll be OK."

Even as I spoke I knew I could not hold out. My strength was gone, but each time the sled went in it came out heavier with ice than before. I had to do something, and fast.

I hopped up, tore open the sled tarp, and dragged out a bag of dog food, a sack of dried fish, traps, bait, marten. I threw everything up a steep bank above the water and jerked the lightened sled up one last time.

"Hike!" I cried. The dogs got it going as I stumbled behind in the darkness. After only a few feet the ice held my weight. I hurried after the team, and when Loki stopped a short distance on I caught up, tipped the sled over and banged the ice off again. The frozen slush fell away in a slippery pile four inches deep and the length of the six-foot sled basket. Once relieved of the weight of both the load and the ice, the sled glided easily over the weak surface and the dogs hurried forward.

The cabin never look so good, cold and bleak though it was. The change of footgear had saved my feet, but every muscle in my back and shoulders twisted and kinked. But I made it, I made it. That was enough. I had run into overflow plenty of times before, in temperatures down to fifty below, but never like this.

I was so tired I could not cook a decent meal so relied on our old standby, a two-quart pot of cocoa made double strength with powdered whole milk and snow-water. In the morning, after the water froze, I could return for my cached load. Meantime I was grateful for the warm little cabin to stay in. Even if it was a bit crowded with six big, wet huskies in it.

When water is sitting on top of the ice instead of soaked into the snow, everything is easier and we can usually press on without difficulty, even across the shin-deep creek where it runs wide open over cobbled stones.

This was the case when Julie and I made a gallant attempt to rescue that little sled we'd abandoned during the spring trip through the park three years earlier. We figured it was only twenty miles up from our Spruce Cabin, and when winter came early with cold weather and little snow, we figured this was the ideal time. We would just scoot up the frozen creek unhampered by deep snow, pick up the battered old sled, and beat it home for dinner.

Such was not the case. First off, I was towing as usual on skis behind Julie's dogsled, and in crossing river bars I managed to rake my knees constantly over the fist-sized cobbles. Then we started hitting overflow. Just a little at first. The dogs trotted blithely through the skim of water glaciering the ice, never slackening their nine-mile-an-hour gait despite the ten-below weather.

As low hills began pressing the creek into a narrow channel, we slipped by rushing open water defying the December temperatures. To add injury to insult, glacial boulders started popping up, two and three feet high, littering the creek bed and threatening to disembowel our sled. One more bend brought us to a spot where the creek ran wide open in a channel which zigzagged from one bank to the other around a wide sandbar.

One spot looked frozen, but as I tiptoed onto the ice I fell into frigid ankle-deep water. My feet, in those confoundedly low ski boots, were instantly drenched. I backtracked hastily, scouted the area from the thickets on the bank, and reported back to Julie.

"We'll have to run the dogs across the water at the lower end of that bar, and again at the top," I told her. "We can't get them through that brush on the bank."

The ice water was eight inches deep and flowing fast. The dogs balked so I grabbed Loki and pitched him in, and he dragged the rest of the team across the rushing channel. The next crossing was wider but shallower and the big black-and-white husky marched right across. The sled splashed through the water, runners dragging on the sandy bottom. Meanwhile, to spare my feet I picked my way through the thicket, avoiding both crossings and meeting Julie at the top.

Half a mile on we ran into more open water. A thin bridge of ice spanned the creek, and although the narrow channel looked deep it was only five feet across. Loki started out bravely, but his feet broke through the treacherous ice. He plunged forward and scrambled out on the opposite side, dragging the next pair of the nine-dog team into the hole.

Those two broke through, but not badly. The remaining dogs weren't so lucky. The ice broke away completely and they fell full into the water, dragged in by the forward dogs. Two by two, each pair slipped scrabbling into the current, to be swept off their feet and held against the rushing water by the straining towline.

By this time Julie decided there was no way she was going across that hip-deep hole. She leaped back as the sled fell in and sank until only the top half of the handlebow showed above the swirling white and black water.

"*Do* something!" she shrieked. Although I was in no better position to help than she, I figured I'd better do something fast because evidently the whole thing was my fault, even though I'd been towing innocently at the tail end of our procession.

(Julie's note: It *was* her fault, because I'd wanted to cross the creek in a shallower spot instead of here.)

Anyway, I darted downstream, searching for a place to get across as Julie scrambled over the boulders upstream. Spying a wide, shallow section, I tore off my skis and bounded across, drenching my feet for a second time. The bush bow of the sled had jammed under the rim of shelf ice and the dogs waited anxiously for me, water dripping and freezing on their coats. I flipped off my mittens, drove my hands into the clear, cold water and hauled the sled up. As soon as the line slackened Loki brought the team forward until the sled stood safely dripping on firm ice.

I exchanged my freezing boots for mukluks, threw my skis into the sled, and trotted behind the team. When the creek narrowed again we found the water wide open and the boulders thickly strewn across the channel. We stopped, built a fire, ate raisins and cocoa and fed the dogs dried fish. Julie checked out the next half-mile and returned to report it nearly impassable. Sun dogs blazed over the mountains, encircling the sun with a weird golden halo, thickening on either side into prismlike rainbow spots.

Loki executed a perfect "Come gee!" He was glad that we had enough sense for once to head for home instead of pushing on under ridiculous and even dangerous conditions toward an uncertain, if worthy, goal. My ski boots, dried by the fire to a sticky dampness, kept my feet warm as we dodged and splashed our way home. Back at the cabin, we welcomed in all nine dogs, icy harnesses and all, and contemplated how that old sled might look after a few more years in the wild.

So much for *that* bright idea.

Since then we've never seen a year of so little snow. Oh, it was a bugger, all right. On river bars, our sleds grated over the cobbles from November until January. River travel was actually easy if we stayed on the ice and didn't tangle with overflow, but traveling over tussocks proved fatal to a couple sleds. Julie once took a full hour to cross a two-mile stretch of trail with a three-hundred-pound load as it tipped and rolled on the rough ground. The first time I broke trail on out from our Birch Cabin the twenty-mile run left me bruised and aching. With a very light load the sled was manageable, but simply staying on the runners was a challenge. One fifty-foot stretch of trail ran through knee-high tussocks. The runners slid between the hairy monsters for a few feet, slammed into an irregular growth, and leaped upward, twisting and crashing down only to repeat the maneuver every minute or two. Tussocks swiped me off the runners time and again, and for seconds I would drag over the rough ground on my knees, clinging to the handlebow as the dogs trotted merrily over the tortured ground.

I thought that was bad enough, but no, five miles on the tussocks grew even bigger, crowding a hundred-yard stretch of trail. The dogs slowed to a careful walk as they picked their way along the tops of the clumps. I could not step off the runners to ease their load without risking a dislocated knee as my foot disappeared into the grassy depths, and even the towline and sled harness snagged up.

By the time I returned to the cabin the sled brake had sheared off and one plastic runner shoe dangled by a single bolt, held in place only by a hasty and ineffective "string job."

"I am *not* going back out there," I snarled as I poured out the day's woes to my unsympathetic sister. "That sled can't go out until the plastic's fixed, and that means a trip home — we haven't any bolts here."

"We have to get the traps set," Julie replied. Setting trail is critical during the first weeks of the trapping season, and she wouldn't believe a word of my troubles.

"I'll take the freight sled out," she offered.

"That thing is so snub-nosed, it'll jam into every little bump."

"No, it won't."

"Yes, it will."

It didn't. Julie departed at dawn with the big sled for the next line cabin, despite my misgivings. The long sled sailed over the muskeg, held up by wide, ten-foot-long runners. But even it was not infallible.

"The runner broke," she reported to me over ham radio that evening. "I might have to walk back."

Walking twenty-seven miles with eight loose huskies provoked interesting thoughts. "I'll call on the radio if I do. You can walk out and meet me," Julie suggested cheerily.

She didn't call. I stewed around the cabin all the next day until I finally heard my leftover dogs leap into a wild chorus of greeting. As I bolted outside the team and sled limped into view.

The runner had snapped off at the very front. Julie had hacked out a splint from a naturally twisted birch sapling, lashed and nailed it in place, and hoped it held. It did. The freighter not only made it back to the cabin, but we put on an additional hundred and fifty miles of rough trail before retiring it for the winter.

We learned a lot about repairing sleds that year. The most important lesson was that a broken sled was not the end of the trail. No matter how frightful a wreck looked, it could always be stuck back together just one more time. Breaks became routine, not calamities. The question put to a tired musher at the end of the day was no longer "How many marten?" It became, "What broke?"

Almost every night at least one sled was crowded into the small cabin for repairs, and a quick fix along the trail became part of the daily chores. Once on a long run the front headboard jiggled loose from a rickety basket. When it fell off completely I figured I'd better do something, since it normally holds the whole front end together. Being in quite a rush and working in the dark, I didn't do more than tie the thing back in (upside-down) just well enough to keep something else from breaking, and boogied on home. The fact that the thermometer registered fifty below when I arrived might have had a bit to do with the haste of my repair job.

That's the way it is on the trapline. Improvising. Ceaseless work. Cold feet. Knowing exactly how far you can safely push yourself, and how to make it right when you reach the end of your physical capabilities. A very deep appreciation for an old pair of mukluks or a dingy, cold cabin with no plumbing, electricity or steady heat. The security of feeling totally at home anywhere along a hundred miles of trail. The faith in one's dogs, one's partner, and one's own abilities.

And always, always, the awareness of natural forces, much bigger and more powerful than my own insignificant self, always out there, always waiting for the one day I forget to pack along that spare pair of mukluks.

# 6

# THE BIRDS AND THE BEES
# AND THE BEARS

rapline chores don't always end with the coming of summer. Nearly every year Julie and I spend some time — a few days, or a few weeks — out on the trapline repairing cabin roofs, building dog houses, picking cranberries or goofing off. Occasionally a line cabin has to be rebuilt or replaced altogether. Slim had ten or more cabins ranging in size from twenty-by-thirty down to six-by-eight hovels one could not rise above a crouch in, but only the big one next to our house at home is still in good condition. Some are totally unusable.

We built the Spruce Cabin, forty-five miles out, at a site where Slim had built at least two cabins, one replacing the other as it rotted and fell in. Julie and Ray cut the logs and started the cabin one summer, but then were interrupted. Two summers later I flew out with Ray to finish the job.

We landed on a tiny lake five miles from the site, and hiked over the spruce-covered hills with heavy packs of food, tools and supplies. Two days of steady rain had turned the muskeg and tundra into soggy muck and swelled the small streams into narrow, roaring torrents. Two streams we crossed using downed trees as precarious bridges. The third, at the cabin site, raged seventy feet wide. Ray crossed first, lining a taut rope across, and then returned for his pack. We crossed gripping the rope, holding ourselves against the rushing water, waves rising to my chest from the force of the current.

The cabin had two and a half of the five rounds of logs already up, and we hoped to finish the work in a week. We camped on the sandbar in front of the cabin, cooked over a campfire and delighted in the fair weather, the more enjoyable since we had only a tarp for protection. I was sound asleep the next morning when I heard Ray shout.

"Hey! Get out of here!"

I jerked my head up. Looking out groggily, I saw him glaring back into the woods from his sleeping bag a few feet away.

"A bear," he said. "Just a small one."

Black bears are not uncommon in this area, and even a few grizzlies wander down occasionally from the higher country. A lot of people who don't know better are terrified of bears. A lot of people who ought to know better aren't afraid of bears at all. I don't go through life dreading a bear encounter, but when I do bump into one I'd just as soon take myself elsewhere without delay. I used to have bear nightmares when I was a little kid. I still have bad bear dreams, but now the villains usually succumb to my rifle so I wake up feeling a little better.

We started work immediately after breakfast, dragging logs to the cabin with the help of a come-along and then lifting them, one end at a time, to the top of the walls. Because Ray planned to use this as his main camp when he came out trapping, he wanted a nice cabin, fourteen-and-a-half by eleven-and-a-half feet, with large logs to hold in the heat and tall walls so we wouldn't have to scrunch down all the time. Moss from the spruce forest chinked the logs. Each round, a foot higher than the one before, became more difficult to raise, but by late evening the walls were up. The following day we built up the ends to allow for the slope of the roof, and cut the door out with the chain saw. Everything progressed smoothly and as we sank into bed that night, snug on the grassy floor of the roofless cabin, we hoped our luck would hold. It was not to be.

Ray was sharpening the bow saw by the campfire on the beach the following morning and I was puttering around picking up after breakfast, when I heard a subtle twig snap back in the trees. Most of the twig-snaps I hear never materialize into anything but I kept my eyes open anyway, and sure enough, a moment later I was shocked to see a good-sized black bear striding across the sandbar, not thirty feet away.

I reached over and gave Ray a hard jab in the back. "Ray! A *bear*!"

He whirled about, spied the intruder and frowned. His rifle was up in the cabin. We both stood up and the bear, not daring to approach the lingering odors of our breakfast while we remained close, went on by. Ray shouted at him and the bear stopped to give us a short glare before walking unhurriedly into the alders.

That's what I don't like, a bear who is not afraid of human scent or sound.

We quickly retrieved Ray's .348 and sneaked after the intruder, catching him just as he headed toward the smell of pancakes again.

Join us for breakfast, Bear, and we'll have you for dinner. But he spied us, wheeled, and lumbered back into the sheltering trees. Ray followed him and a moment later two warning shots cracked out. Ray reappeared with a grin on his face.

"I walked up fifteen feet from him," he told me. "He went '*Whoof*' and jumped five feet toward me. I pointed the gun at him and said, 'Do that again, Bear!'"

"Did he run when you shot?"

"Yeah. I hope he doesn't come back."

Five minutes later I started up to the cabin and practically bumped right into him coming out of the bushes. We both jumped back, startled, and made hasty retreats, the bear into the gloomy alders, me back to the safety of Ray's weapon. Moments later we heard him within the cabin walls where my pack of food lay.

Ray and I ran up the bank and the bear poked his head out of the doorway, stared for a moment, and then went back inside. We started slipping around to the back of the cabin, fearing if we blocked the doorway the bear might feel trapped and charge. When we were a few feet from the cabin the bear, without warning, leaped to the top of the five-foot wall as easily as a cat leaps onto a chair. He stood poised on the top for a moment, looking around, and then dropped over the side and trotted a short distance away.

Inside the cabin we found the pack torn open and a box of rice scattered in the grass. I looked over the wall and saw the thief standing fifty yards away, eyeing us.

"I'm going to get some rocks," Ray said.

Hurling stones at some shady character was not something I would have relished, but I didn't protest as Ray hurried toward the beach. As soon as he'd gone the bear began moving toward the cabin as I watched over the wall. He paused just fifteen feet away, front paws standing on a log, each long claw etched against the wood as he stared myopically at me. He started forward again just as Ray returned.

The bear disappeared behind the tall back wall, only a few feet away, and we moved warily to the middle of the enclosure. At any moment we expected him to leap to the top of the wall again, and we could only guess where. After a tense moment I peeked over one wall and saw the bear glaring at me just seven feet away.

"He's here," I hissed as the bear edged forward and then retreated again. Ray came to my side, handed me the rifle, and sent a fist-sized stone rocketing into the bear's shoulder.

The bear whirled away and leaped back as another rock shot past his rump, backed up with an angry shout. Fifty feet away the bear stopped again and turned back. Ray and I exchanged uneasy glances. That bear obviously intended to stay around until he got a decent meal — and once that happened, he'd hang around until the food ran out.

"I think you'd better shoot him," I said grimly. Neither of us wanted to take the time to butcher a bear, but he was bound to become a hazard. If we didn't shoot him now, we almost surely would have to later, maybe after he'd eaten our precious supply of food or even attacked one of us.

Ray walked toward him and the bear stood unafraid, a little belligerent, as Ray leaned against a tree, aimed with a sure hand and fired.

We spent the rest of the afternoon skinning and cleaning the bear. Although it proved to be a large bear it had little meat and no fat. The poor berry season probably contributed to his ornery, hungry behavior. Ray built a rack and put an old half-drum stove under it while I cut the meat into thin strips for drying. Every morning after that I lit the fire and kept it burning slowly all day.

Work on the cabin progressed steadily after that interruption. The ridgepole went in, and then the split-pole roof, followed by a layer of Visqueen and a foot of moss. A year later Ray added more Visqueen and another thick layer of moss for added insulation. We moved the rusty old stove in from Slim's old cabin; it would do until we could get a better one. With the chain saw Ray cut rough planks from a large spruce and constructed a bed, table and shelves. With a warm fire roaring in the stove to drive the moisture from the cabin, Ray and I stepped back to survey our work. I grinned as Ray gave his characteristic "Heh, heh, heh!" of satisfaction. The completed cabin stood warm and solid despite our inexperience and the intrusive bear.

We have been lucky in our bear encounters; they have been few and far between, and those we do run into have rarely caused problems beyond tearing up the trapping cabins every summer. I have had only one really bad scare.

Julie and I were sleeping soundly in our small tent at Moose Camp when it happened. I had shot a moose late the night before and had been out until nearly midnight gutting him, and although the hot September morning beat down on the tent, deep sleep still gripped me.

It was a frightful sound that woke me, the sound of vicious, determined claws ripping and tearing on the roof of the tent, beating a tattoo down the side.

I grabbed the .308, sat up, and had a shell in the chamber and the safety off before I knew what was happening. All I really thought was whether I'd be able to shoot a bear through the wall of the tent, when Julie was lying between me and it. I glanced at her. She was staring at me.

"It was a grouse," she said.

The fool hen had landed on the roof of the tent and skittered down the slippery surface, its clawed feet trying frantically to get a grip on the fabric.

"Oh," I said. I reengaged the safety, took the shell out

of the chamber, and lay down, but I didn't sleep again, and I didn't stop trembling for a long time.

That's about the height of my wild-bear horror tales, in spite of a lifetime in the bush.

Bears were only part of the problem one summer when we put up a lot fish. The gillnets were doing unusually well and a thousand whitefish, suckers, pike and cod weighted down the pole rack, drying for winter dog food.

The wasps found the fish first. We saw more yellow jackets that summer than ever before or since. On a calm evening they covered the drying fish, tails wiggling as they packed in side-by-side, each one stripping off chunks of flesh to carry back to the nest for the rapidly multiplying larvae. At first we didn't think much of it, but when we found some fish stripped down to the skin, Ray and Julie and I decided the time had come to wage war.

Julie and I were fifteen then, Ray a year and a half older, all three ready for adventure of the most hazardous kind. Our campaign consisted of systematically searching out and methodically destroying the underground nests. Dressed in heavy clothes, gloves and headnets, we attacked at night when the chill made the bees sluggish. Our favorite ploy was to pour diesel fuel down the hole, light it, and beat a panicky retreat, laughing and shrieking, until the ensuing uproar ceased and we could return to dig out the remainder in relative safety.

The most delightful attack was on a hanging nest constructed of grayish wasp paper built delicately around a tree branch. Although these aerial nests can be a foot or more in diameter, this one consisted of only six inches of paper and explosive contents. Ray sneaked up on it, shotgun resting easily over one forearm. At ten feet he raised the gun, aimed, and fired. An explosion, followed by a small shower of shredded wasp paper, announced the instant and complete demise of one wasp nest. We destroyed about twenty nests, but whether our campaign against the wasps had much effect remained open to debate.

No sooner had we gained the upper hand over every nest within two hundred yards of the fish rack, than the camp robbers moved in. They flitted here and there, picking off large pieces of fish and gobbling greedily, loading up to later regurgitate the bounty at selected caches high in the birch trees. Now, waging war against swarming, buzzing, stinging yellow jackets and wasps is one thing, but shooting down soft little gray birdies is quite another.

Nevertheless the fish had to be protected, and Ray did pick off a few jays with a .22 in hope of discouraging the rest. With unfailing curiosity I autopsied one, and to my surprise I found the stomach packed not with fish but with wasps! After that the birds stayed, although we could see them daily stripping the fish of meat as well as insects.

For awhile the ravens moved in. They arrived daily at five a.m., screaming and yelling, destroying the fish and leaving what they did not eat or pack away scattered across the beach.

One morning as they swooped in for their breakfast I crept outside, clad in pink pajamas and packing Daddy's shotgun. One blast into the raucous early morning party brought an instant silence as the big black birds dropped from the tree and soared swiftly away. I'd forgotten we had company sleeping in the old cabin next door, and I'm sure I don't know what they thought if they peeked out the window and saw me standing on the porch at that early hour, pink pajamas billowing, shotgun smoldering, and a smirk on my sleepy face.

Despite that sudden attack the ravens persisted, but an old fish net hung around the rack finally discouraged them and their early-morning coffee klatches petered out.

Then the bears moved in.

Pingo alerted us to the first arrival early one morning. Our little pet of many years awoke us, not with her customary alarm bark but with a low, throaty growl. Julie peered groggily out the window, and down by the fish rack she spied a large black shape.

"A bear!" she roared. "There's a bear in the fish rack!"

Our house exploded into disunited action. Our parents were in Fairbanks but we three kids thundered downstairs, Ray snatching up his .348 as he ran. Our noise frightened the intruder away, but several hours later it returned — a large black sow. This time the alert was sounded more quietly and Ray slipped out to fire a deafening shot over the bear's head, speeding her departure tenfold. We hoped that would end the problem.

It didn't. There were actually three bears. The sow never came back, but her two yearling cubs began raiding our fish nightly. Shooting over their heads scared them off, but the tantalizing odor of sweet, sun-dried fish lured them back time and again, usually at night but sometimes in the day as well.

"Poor Kitty," I cried after Ray once again speeded the exit of one bear. Our cat had hurried up from the beach, her tail big and straight as a baseball bat. She'd stood up to sled dogs and foxes, but a bear was a bit much.

When the nightly raids became more frequent and the fish began disappearing at an alarming rate, we decided the bears had to go. The August nights were getting darker when Ray settled down on the porch for a night's sentry duty, his .348 across his knees.

He heard the bear rather than saw it. In the gloom he just made out the black form under the fish. Running to the edge of the bank above the fish rack, he stopped and fired twice, shocking the rest of the household into heart-pounding alertness.

Marmee, now home from Fairbanks, yelled out the window. "Shoot him again, Ray!"

Another shot obediently boomed out and echoed across the bay and up the hill, resounding in the darkness and ending for all time one small bear with a fatal taste for fish. Everyone tumbled out of bed to help butcher him by the light of a lantern. The meat, untainted by the fish he'd consumed, was tender if not exactly flavorful. Luckily his sibling did not return, and our fish at last dried in relative peace and quiet — until we hung the dry bales in the cache and the squirrels started in on them.

Running the fish nets is a daily chore, from the time they are set in the spring until the shelf ice threatens to seal them in as October presses on. Our favorite site is on a long spit two miles from our house, and the four-mile paddle in the canoe gives us the chance to run a few dogs loose on the beach. They learn quickly to head for the net, wait on the beach while we pull out the fish, and then trot home again.

All goes well until some wild thing presents itself, and the dogs take off for an afternoon of fun and frolic, running who-knows-where after God-knows-what. Only occasionally are we privileged to watch the fun.

Loki and Tok once chased a cow moose with twin calves on the beach for a couple of hours. Moose usually head for water when threatened, and Ma Moose herded her little ones in until they stood chest deep while she held the attackers at bay. The dogs feinted in until she charged, sending spray high above her six-foot shoulders as she drove them back to the beach. She never followed them far, afraid of leaving her calves open to a flank attack. One sharp hoof caught old Tok in the shoulder and he backed off until we crept close enough to catch him. Loki held out until, in his overbearing, aggressive manner, he ran too far out in the water. He couldn't turn fast enough and she caught him, her front feet pounding him beneath the churning water.

Miraculously he came out unscathed but wiser for the experience. After a few more half-hearted feints he too allowed us to catch him.

Trapper, the big malemute, was a confirmed moose hunter, and while at times his bravado was all bluff, when it came to moose he didn't know when to quit. He and another malemute, Yukon, caught a barren cow one summer day as we headed home in the canoe from the spit, and the fight was on.

An enraged cow will charge with a roar or a growl which makes one think more of a grizzly than an oversized deer. This impressive sound up in the trees on the hill announced the opening round of the fray. We heard the thud of hooves and Trapper yelling.

"Get Yukon!" I cried, hauling the bow of the canoe around toward the shore. We paddled like fiends, trying to head him off, but too late! The hundred-pound idiot was heading for the ruckus as fast as his uncoordinated legs could carry him.

The moose hit the water running, with Trapper hot on her heels. Without calves she was not so aggressive, but neither was she tied to one spot, as her charges were not limited by the concern of leaving little ones unprotected. She waded into flank-deep water and Trapper plunged in after her, swimming furiously. Yukon followed some distance behind, unsure but determined to follow Trapper. We crowded as close as we dared, hoping to drive the cow on down the beach so we could overtake the dogs, but just as we were about to swoop in on Yukon the moose headed right for us and we beat a hasty retreat.

She moved back and forth along the beach, trying to stay out of deeper water farther along, where the shore dropped off quickly. When she did move into deeper water she was almost swimming. Once again she turned with grim determination toward shallow water, but Yukon, ahead for once, was closing in.

Yukon was thrilled. He was actually going to catch himself a moose! Suddenly the cow reared up and charged him. Quickly he turned tail and began swimming away. He swam as fast as he could. His eyes popped with the effort as he tried to swim and look back at this monster bearing down on him.

She charged past, bouncing him off one shoulder. The water was too deep for her to hit him with her sharp hooves as she rushed on by.

Trapper intended to head her off, but she made for shore. Both were in somewhat shallower water when the cow charged Trapper, and Trapper, still swimming, charged the cow. Neither hesitated an instant and when they connected Trapper went down under her churning legs. He went clear under her, not surfacing until she'd already charged on down the beach, some distance away and traveling fast.

Julie and I swooped in and grabbed Trapper's tail as he started swimming blindly for the moose again. Julie headed for safer waters, countering Trapper's powerful strokes only by effort, until I got hold of his ruff and heaved the sodden eighty-five-pound weight into the boat.

He was unhurt, but I found moose hairs stuck between his front teeth. He hadn't let that old cow stomp all over *him* without getting in at least one bite.

Friends in town frequently ask, "What do you do out there in the bush?"

"We trap," we say, even though this answer is misleading since that occupies only four or five months of the year. The rest of the time we spend just living.

Bush life makes demands unknown to city folk. We must grow, gather catch or shoot most of our food. We must provide our own water, electricity, heat and transportation. So we have to buy or build equipment, not to mention maintaining and repairing it because repairmen aren't to be found.

I am by no means a mechanical genius, but Daddy is. When he is at home he maintains the boat motors, snow machine and planes, water pumps, solar and wind and diesel power plants, battery-operated chest freezer, propane stove, wood furnace and creaky old Maytag washing machine and clothes wringer. As the need arises he also cuts firewood, hauls gas, operates the ham radio, and acts as plumber, welder, electrician, carpenter, engineer and mechanic.

Marmee undertakes the worst chores uncomplaining: housekeeping, washing, cooking and worrying. The worrying is the most important part. *Somebody* has to do it, and she does it best. Any time we go somewhere, whether to pick berries, hunt moose, or spend a week on the trapline, we file a "flight plan" with her — where we're going, when we'll be back, and when to start worrying. Help might be as close as the nearest telephone, but when that phone is forty miles back down the trail it's good to know someone reliable is keeping tabs on us!

Julie and I spend the off-seasons concentrating on caring for the dogs, the garden, and our business. By business we mean earning enough cash to tide us over until the next fur check. We make handcrafts to sell, and that combined with a little money from freelance writing and photography usually sees us from the end of the last fur check to the next one, although September and October can be a little lean. But most of the time is spent just doing chores. The nets must be checked and the fish cooked daily with rice; dogsleds, houses, harnesses and lines made or repaired, dog yard kept clean, vaccines and wormings updated, pups cared for and wounds treated.

Next to the dogs and financial endeavors, the garden probably requires the most time. In April we plant some seeds inside to pre-start them and in late May or early June the garden is plowed and planted. Then it must be weeded and fertilized regularly, squeezing everything possible out of the ninety days during which we can hope for frost-free growing. We build pea fences, hill miles of potatoes, and ring the garden with chicken wire to keep out nibbling bunnies and galloping dogs.

By mid-July the harvest is started and every day we blanch and freeze broccoli, cauliflower, peas and chard. The work increases by leaps and bounds as berries ripen, and we pick and freeze or jam gallons and gallons of raspberries, blueberries, currants and cranberries. I can pint after pint of rhubarb, whitefish and, later, moose meat, and dry parsley for seasoning during the long winter.

Before the ground freezes hard in September the root vegetables have to be pulled, cured and packed in the root cellar. The carrots will be blanched and frozen in late October when winter provides unlimited freezer space. Beets are pickled, but in the root cellar our potatoes — up to eight hundred pounds of them — will last until the following summer.

Moose-hunting marks the climax of the fall harvest. Every year we make a determined effort to shoot one moose. Just one will last the four of us a full year, stretched with a little fish, small game and store-bought meat. Ray was only thirteen when he began hunting regularly with Daddy and shot his first moose. Julie shot her first one under Ray's guidance the year before we graduated from college.

The next year it was my turn, only Ray was back in school, Daddy was elsewhere, and Julie was nursing a bad head cold. She gamely helped me paddle the canoe on the seven-hour trip to our upper moose camp, but then it was up to me to go out there and bring down the meat.

My jeans, wet over the knees from wading through the deep, grassy sloughs, began to itch by late evening as I plodded around looking for a bull. I had been hunting for only three hours, but in half an hour darkness would be falling, and I still had a mile of swamp and slough to cover to get back to camp where Julie waited. After the long paddle in the morning followed by all that stomping around in the Moose Pasture, I was ready to call it quits until the following dawn.

Shushy-shush . . . Thumpy-thumpy-thump-thump thump.

The soft sound just in the willows from the slough brought me to a silent halt. I don't know why some moose can sound just like a running hare — and the other way around. I honestly didn't know which it was. I was tired. I wanted to go back to camp. But I didn't. I tiptoed after that little sound. And it tiptoed away again. Thumpy-thumpy-thump.

I began to hurry, trotting in the clearer areas. Then I heard it splashing through water, and my heart really started pounding. Bunnies do not splash through water.

The smell of the swamp filled my nostrils with its rich scents. Ahead I heard the moose again, splashing through another shallow pool. If it crossed the main slough I'd either have to swim across or waste precious time looking for a beaver dam to cross on, and with mid-September bringing freezing nights, swimming had little appeal.

Then the sound of raking antlers came to me, bone against brush, slashing, bending and stripping the willows as a bull announced his awesome presence. I moved forward quickly, breaking out of the alders onto the edge of a small swamp. Beyond the clearing I spied the top of a fifteen-foot alder waving madly as the bull rubbed his antlers. My heart began to pound again, the wind sucking into my lungs as I took a slow, deep breath.

Somehow the barrel of my .308 scraping a dry willow did not sound so impressive as the great smashing of the bull's antlers, but the .308 was all I had. Silence fell on the swamp, and as the colder breeze brought the cool scent of stagnant water, the bull began moving around the swamp toward me, slowly, hidden in the darkening brush.

A small dried slough led out of the end of the swamp. The moose would reach it and either follow it toward me or cross it to disappear almost instantly in the dense growth. I stopped, half-hidden in willows, and pushed the safety off.

The moose moved forward steadily now. All was very still except for the slight tinkling, brushing sound of his antlers sliding through the willows.

There! Oh, Lord, he was big. A massive gray-white antler broke out of the low trees, swinging ponderously as its mate materialized.

He paused, hesitating. The willows, even in the slough, rose to his eyes, and I didn't have a clear shot. If he crossed the slough I'd never have a chance.

He didn't. He moved forward, directly toward me. I lifted the rifle slowly. A chest shot. This is not what I wanted, a chest shot through the trees. I didn't dare try for a head shot. The sun was gone, the daylight lingering.

Now I could see his chest, still partially obscured by the willows which cluttered my view. Then he stopped and stared, knowing I was there but unconcerned. He swung his head, the massive antlers painting a wide arc as he glanced behind him and then toward the willows across the little slough.

I knew that look. He was going to leave. I leveled the rifle, aimed carefully. The branches blurred his chest, but in another moment he'd be gone.

The sound of the shot shook through me. My shoulder cried unheard from the kick. The bull leaped, twirled and disappeared before I could even sight the rifle again, and I snapped off another shot, desperately, as our winter's meat supply vanished into the willows.

I ran. Oh, I ran! The breath was choking in me. My legs were weak and shaking as I sprinted through the willows and over the boggy ground. This was worse than not getting a moose at all. The scent of him, heavy, thick, a little nauseating, filled my throat. Had I hit him? Would he go down perhaps miles away in a thicket where I'd never find him if I searched for a million years?

Then I heard him splashing steadily not far ahead. He was crossing the main slough.

In a few minutes I wouldn't be able to see the sights clearly. I'd have to swim the slough, trying to hold the rifle above my head.

I broke out of the willows, and as the open slough stretched out in front of me, I saw him. He had stopped to stand broadside to me, head up, gazing back. I must have missed him completely. He wasn't afraid. He thought the stretch of water between us made him as safe as it would if I'd been a wolf or bear.

I raised the rifle. I would not miss this time. This was the last chance. I aimed carefully down the dim open sights. This time I was too scared and too determined to tremble.

The shot rang out, echoed from the low hill, cried out into the cool, damp dusk. The bull reared slightly on his hind legs. The massive rack jerking back over his shoulders as he rolled to the ground.

I shot twice more to be sure he wasn't going to move before I could reach him. If he traveled even a few feet into the willows I might not find him in the deepening darkness.

I found a beaver dam several hundred feet upstream. The water came well over my boots but I was already wet and didn't care. The stars peeked out as I jogged back down the slough. I hoped the bull wouldn't be hidden in the tall grass.

He wasn't. He lay still where he'd fallen, on the marshy bank of the slough. I knew Julie would have heard the shots and she'd be on her way with the lantern, packs, bone saw and rope.

I fired signal shots to give her my location and started

to work gutting the moose.

I've heard tell a deer can be cleaned in a few minutes and packed out whole. This sounds a bit incredible to someone who has grown up butchering deer weighing half to three-quarters of a ton. I heaved the hind leg up to expose the abdomen, trying to brace it out of the way while I started to slit the belly, working mostly by feel.

Julie took forever to reach me. I yelled myself hoarse trying to direct her when she crossed to the wrong side of the slough and had to backtrack to the beaver dam. Finally I heard her coming, boots squishing softly in the grassy mud.

"I got him," I called, a little jubilant.

"Right." She knew, of course. She had heard the shots.

"He's big."

"Good." All the more meat for the freezer.

With rope, another pair of hands and light from the lantern, the job went faster. I was wet and cold, bloody to the elbows, tired from the long day's work, proud I had shot a big moose, ashamed to have missed him the first time. The seat of my jeans was wet and a little bloody from the time I sat down on the broad side of the bull to rest.

A dense fog formed in the freezing temperatures later in the night, dampening our clothes and stinging our fingers until we warmed them in the hot gut cavity. Our shadows, formed by the bright lantern light, were flung towering into the sky against the fog droplets and a background of twinkling stars, and beyond the black willows skulked countless imaginary bears.

Only after the guts lay steaming in a separate pile on the ground and the body cavity was relatively clean did we stop and rest, warming ourselves over a sluggish fire built on the sodden ground. By the time the light began to seep back into the sky we had started butchering the meat, placing the big pieces carefully on the hide to keep them clean.

We each packed a light load the half-mile through the willows along the slough, over the scrub-spruce hill with its deep, wet moss and stickery branches, and down to the river. We stashed the meat on the bank and found our way back to camp just as the sun broke over the horizon, shining softly off the silty-gray water of the shallow river.

Julie slept until three in the afternoon, but by noon the sun was beating down on the tent and I lay wide awake, thinking about that pile of meat under the hot sun, about the flies and the (maybe) bears, and finally I crept out, stiff and still groggy. I walked slowly across the hill back to the moose, where I found it free of both flies and bears. I packed one load out, and then we both returned and finished butchering the meat.

The antlers were big and broad. When I tipped them on end the left tines reached well above my head, while the right tines sank into the mud below my feet. I am five-foot-five, so the antlers must have been sixty-eight to seventy-two inches across. I was proud of that rack, but we had no use for those handsome antlers. We left them there in the swamp, and even today I can fly out there and see them, bleached white against the brown-green of the marsh.

We packed meat until evening, hauling up to eighty pounds each. With those loads we didn't want to pack the rifle back and forth, but because of the bear sign in the area we left it in the trees a couple of hundred feet from the meat in case we startled a bear on the kill. Sure enough, when we returned the next morning the rifle had been knocked over and the case chewed on. A bear had eaten about twenty pounds of suet, but left the meat in good shape. After that we carried the rifle everywhere, despite its extra weight.

We had planned on making two trips with the canoe to get the meat home, but after the bear came we decided to try it in one trip. With eight hundred pounds of meat plus our camping and hunting gear, we'd be overloading the eighteen-foot canoe, but Julie and I had a considerable amount of experience with the little craft and we knew the river by heart. We had confidence in ourselves and our craft.

We set off downriver with four inches of freeboard. Everything was carefully tied in place and the canoe balanced perfectly, side to side and fore to aft. Even if we did tip over the river rarely came over our waists, although the thought of trying to rescue all that meat in a swamped canoe was sobering.

The river is fed from glaciers. It runs with swirling gray ice water only sixty miles from its source. In the cooler fall temperatures the melt-off was reduced and the river began dropping rapidly. Every mile or two we ran aground, and we stepped out into the cold water, sinking several inches into the sand, to pull the canoe to deeper water. Our boots were just in the way so we went barefoot, drenched above the knees.

The delta was the worst. As it hits the calm lake water, the river drops its load of silt, forming a wide, long bar. We waded back and forth in the cold water for ten minutes before finding a channel barely deep enough to squeak the canoe through.

The sun was setting behind our hill as we slowly paddled the last half-mile. The scent of wood smoke reached our nostrils, mingling with the wet of the lake and the smell of fresh meat, all mixing with the red-gold reflections of the sunset and the softly lapping waves against the bow of the canoe to create a growing euphoria. Marmee would have dinner ready; Daddy would help hang the meat in the screened-off shed. Our meat! A year's worth of stew and roast, ribs and steak, bones for the huskies, suet to render, scraps for the jays. Liver for dinner tomorrow.

I was very happy.

# 7

# MOOSE, MORE BEARS AND ROTTEN ICE

"We're going to get him Wednesday night," Miki said as we lay in camp one gloomy fall day during our yearly moose hunt.

"We're going to hunt all day today and not get one?" I asked.

"Yup."

"Go *on*."

"Bet."

"How much?" I asked.

"A million dollars," Miki said.

"Hundred thousand." I wasn't going to lose all the million I'd won on the last bet.

"OK."

Miki and I stared out the tent door at a light drizzle drifting onto the river by the mud bar. It was noon and we felt washed up. We had arrived yesterday after a hard eight-hour paddle up the fast, silty stream. We'd hunted moose last night, and again at dawn today.

I don't mind walking through wet brush, across soggy marshes or narrow beaver dams. I rather like tiptoeing through willows three inches apart, sneaking through the woods, quietly listening, chewing on a straw. I picked that up from Ray. Chewing straws has a sedative effect.

What I don't like is the pressure of moose hunting. What if we don't get one this year? For those who live in the bush, this is critical, not because we need another trophy but because our whole year's meat supply depends upon our luck during the short fall hunting season. This isn't a matter of pride or tradition, it's a matter of economy. After paying exorbitant prices for grocery meat, we'd have to add on another thirty-five cents a pound for the air freight to get it home.

By that Wednesday night, with the time limit on Miki's bet fast approaching, I began wondering what we'd do if we failed to shoot a moose. We had several days of hunting left and there were plenty of bulls around, but I still felt nervous. The longer it takes to shoot a moose, the more nervous I get. I spent the afternoon cruising the long, swampy creek back of camp, just watching and waiting, standing on the bank in the willows and the mosquitoes, chewing a straw to bits and then moving on.

Miki was off somewhere alone. It's hard hunting together. When the lead hunter spots a moose and begins the stalk with intense concentration, the back-up usually starts giggling. It happens almost every time. So I work alone.

I heard a twig snap a long way off. Then a faint thump. At least it was a noise, so I started creeping toward it. Then a moose began grunting — small, sporadic groans growing to great belches which sound like a bear throwing up. He was walking toward me, so I waited for him. Every yard he moved was one yard less we'd have to pack him to the canoe.

Finally I saw the tall willows whipping about as he thrust his antlers against them. He came nearer, head down, getting uncomfortably close without showing himself. At last he raised his head, his face and antlers framed by willows, hardly thirty feet from me. I steadied the .308 and fired. He stood gazing at me. I was so surprised when he didn't move, I just stood staring. How could I have missed?

Then he crumpled to the ground, dead. Miki had won her bet, but I didn't care. The pressure was off — we had meat for the pot. This winter we would eat stew, barbecued ribs, sweet-and-sour steak, liver and onions, pot roasts, oven roasts, meat and potatoes, and hamburger made into chili, spaghetti sauce, pizza and tacos.

A lot of hard, bloody work followed in gutting and quartering and packing the meat out, but it was gratifying labor. Only on the first trip out in the dark, we had some trouble. Miki tripped on the beaver dam, splattered herself across the swamp, and rolled around shrieking and shouting with that whopping slab of ribs squishing her into the muck.

We couldn't manage more than a hundred pounds per pack, which meant several loads each. As usual, by the time we got all the meat out we couldn't care less about the handsome rack. Besides, with all that meat, us two and our camping gear in the eighteen-foot canoe, we were lucky to get down the shallow river without getting wet. I mean, without getting *too* wet.

Most years, moose hunting goes all right. Sometimes it rains. When it doesn't rain, the no-see'ums come out. But so far as the hunting goes, we generally get lucky. One year we hunted right up to the last day without luck. Near dusk on the last day of the season we stopped at one last marsh and I saw Miki's eyes pop out as she peeped through the tight trees. Turning swiftly to me, she flashed her spread hand up to her head, imitating moose antlers.

I didn't believe her. "A bull?" I hissed. She nodded, eyes sparkling. "Are you *sure* it's a bull?" I hissed. How lucky can you get?

Miki nodded again, and turned to begin her stalk. Following in her toe-tracks, I started snickering. I tried clamping my hand over my mouth and nose, but I couldn't stop. Miki, intent on the little bull, ignored me. A few minutes later, despite my tomfoolery, the moose lay dead near the river, and by midnight we were skimming across the lake in the moonlight with a boatload of meat.

A couple of years ago we were hunting back in a willow-choked swamp when I heard a moose not far off. "I hear a moose up there, let's go this way," I whispered.

"That's not a moose," Miki told me. "That's the river, I know. The river can sound like a moose doing anything, walking in the trees or the water or the swamp, or beating his antlers, or running away, or getting up — lying down — piddling — giving birth —"

"I *know* it's a moose!" I shouted in a whisper. "Now let's go get him!" Rolling her eyes, Miki followed me toward the faint splashing sounds. This better be a moose, I thought. Miki usually guessed right. My pride was at stake.

It *was* a moose, a small bull ambling across a slough. I gave Miki my best sneer and she made an ugly face. We stood there sticking our tongues out at each other until the moose came close and then we sneaked over and shot him.

He went down in ten inches of water. As one of my boots leaked I used the canoe as the spare boot, one foot in the water and the other wobbling in the canoe. We cut off the top quarters, ribs and neck, keeping the lower half dry with the hide, and then with the mighty effort we hoisted the rest of the carcass into the canoe and pushed off for camp.

We were heading for shallow water, the canoe riding low, just as a small squally storm hit with wind and rain. "Go that way!" Miki shouted, swinging the bow to the left.

"No, no, to the right," I insisted, shoving to the right from the stern. The canoe wobbled uncertainly and ended up ramming the sandbar dead ahead.

"I told you!" Miki said.

"No, *I* told *you*!" I retorted. More bemused than angry, we pulled and poked and prodded until, just as the rain ended, we were free. We brought one load of meat all the way home and returned to camp for the night, planning to bring the rest out next day. With no trees to tie the canoe to, we simply pulled it forty feet from the water so gusty winds wouldn't roll it all the way into the river.

Next day — "Halloo! Canoe's gone!" Miki cried from the riverbank.

"What? What!" I thundered from the tent, staring wildly around. The current had battered away at the soft mud bank, eating up those forty feet in the night and sucking away our only transportation. On the river's edge, only the imprint of the bow remained over the cut bank.

I threw my prized fur hat furiously onto the mud and quelled the urge to stomp on it. Then we went galloping off downriver in the mud and the wind and the sleet, and finally found our trusty craft hung up in some willows five miles away. Miki stripped and bravely plunged into the frigid water, which was hardly sixty miles from its glacier source.

"Oh!" she gasped. "Come on in, the water's fine!"

After retrieving the errant canoe, we faced a tough paddle against the current and a driving wind and rain storm. Arriving cold and wet at camp, we threw the dry wood we'd cached under the tent fly into a pile and stacked wet wood on top. Pouring on a generous swig of Blazo lantern fuel, Miki struck a match and we warmed right up in the ensuing explosion.

Between all these sallies into the Moose Pasture, we're stuck with chores. The garden needs to be harvested. Driftwood needs to be hauled and stacked for cooking dog food during the winter, and firewood for the wood stoves needs to be hauled when snow comes. Old dogsleds need repairing, and new ones need to be constructed, and winter clothing — fur mukluks, mitts, hats and overpants — needs to be made. We never seem to have time for our favorite job — picking cranberries.

I dream of picking cranberries on cold winter days on the trapline. I dream of sitting in the warm sun at the crest of a bluff overlooking the lake, while great handfuls of firm red berries roll into the bowl. Berries for jam and sweet bread and pancakes. Berries for coffeecake and meat sauces and lemon-cranberry-custard pie.

I dream of picking cranberries when I'm withering in the hot sun gathering raspberries, or fighting gnats in the strawberry patch, or mosquitoes in the blueberry patches. I dream about pulling off handfuls of berries while the sun slips golden through the fall birch leaves, while the dogs lounge in the Labrador tea and listen for mice, while a bald eagle soars overhead, chirping and shrugging off pestering sparrows.

Sadly, it's not always like this. By the time the moose is shot and the potatoes are in, it usually starts to rain. Sometimes, though, we can squeeze in an afternoon of cranberry-picking during good weather. Some dogs come along too, so they can pack the harvest home. They seem to enjoy rolling in the best patches of berries.

The sun grows warmer. A few no-see'ums come out, then a few more. Then lots. And I usually forget the bug dope. I don't care. Cranberry-picking is great, as long as we're not picking in the snow.

Sometimes cranberry-picking can get exciting, but not very often. Once, just once, we were headed for the patch when the dogs roused a black bear eating our berries. Judging by the huffing and puffing and roars and snarls and crashes, they had a good old time before the dogs tired of the sport and came home.

That same year we encountered another bear right by our house. Returning after a couple of hours at the post office to meet the mail plane, we found grizzly tracks on the beach near the dog yard.

"Holy moly!" Miki said.

"Oh, my goodness!" I said. The bear had touched nothing, but with moose meat hanging in the shed and fish drying on the racks, he might return.

I always figured September nights are the darkest of the year, for the sun has taken up its winter quarters already but no white blanket of snow has come to reflect the little available starlight. And it was a cloudy, moonless September night when the grizzly returned.

I took the .264 down from the wall. "Are you sure we want to do this?"

"Scared?" Miki challenged me from across the dark doorway. Outside, in the blackness, the roaring of our chained sled dogs filled the night with pandemonium.

"This isn't a rinky-dink black bear we're talking about," I retorted.

"Do you want to lose all that fish?" Miki demanded, checking her .308.

"I'm coming, I just don't think it's a very good idea."

The grizzly sloshed steadily through two feet of water in the bay. The loud, regular splashing sounded over the cacophony from our dog yard. Half the dogs wanted to kill the bear and the other half, the young ones, were scared to death of it. Miki fired over the bear's head a couple of times, fire flashing from the rifle barrel. I stood ready with my own weapon in case the grizzly took offense. For a frightful moment he turned toward us and we couldn't tell his intentions in the darkness. Then he sloshed off at a pace only slightly increased by the shots.

We carried a rifle for many weeks afterward, although we knew if a grizzly was serious in an attack, like as not you'd never get a shell in the chamber if he caught you by surprise. October nights weren't so dark as nights in September because of a sheet of snow, but one overcast evening darkness caught us as we walked with some dogs, searching for a wayward pair who had run off that morning. We tromped over the snowy rocks near the black water, calling occasionally for the runaway dogs, Sky and Streak. Not far from home, something huge came crashing down the steeply sloped hill. We thought it was Streak, who's pretty darn big, because this animal was bounding straight at us. In the darkness it looked just like Streak — Streak or a bear. By the time we realized it wasn't Streak, we didn't have time to do a thing.

The beast was just a few feet away and moving fast when it veered abruptly, plunged into the freezing water, and swam swiftly away into the darkness.

Well! You can be sure Streak would never do such a thing. But would a bear? I didn't think so. Yet the animal had been too small for a moose. Still puzzled, we resolved to return the next morning and look for tracks. Unfortunately, while we were feeding the dogs (including the errant Sky and Streak, who returned for supper) a heavy snowfall began.

"Let's go back now before this snow covers the tracks," Miki suggested. "We'll bring two guns, the headlamp, and Comet." Comet weighs a hundred and twenty pounds. He's no coward, but he isn't the kind of dog who looks for trouble, either.

Miki's headlamp gleamed on the freshly falling snow as we tromped back to the spot. "I see two eyes glowing up there," she said suddenly. I looked, but the beam of light wasn't at the right angle for me to see the reflecting eyes.

"It's just Comet," I assured her.

"No, I don't think so."

"Sure it is. Comet, Comet, come here."

"Comet's eyes aren't a foot apart," Miki told me.

Comet came trotting up from behind. "It isn't Comet," I said in a hollow voice. As we moved closer I saw the eyes too, big eyes like a fawn's, glowing yellow-green in the light. "Comet, stay with us," I ordered. He did. We sneaked closer to those glowing eyes, rifles ready.

It was a calf moose, lying in the water by the beach, icy waves breaking and freezing on the thick hair of his back. He lay motionless, staring at us with those big crystalline eyes. "Now what?" I wondered. "Is he hurt or exhausted, or just scared?"

"I don't know, but we're not going near him tonight," Miki said. "His mother could be anywhere nearby. Let's come back tomorrow in the light and try to help him if he's still here."

"Right," I agreed. "Comet, let's go."

The next morning the calf was gone and we never knew whether he survived and found his mother again.

We had a different kind of experience with a much smaller animal during one fall freeze-up. A university scientist asked us to live-trap some muskrats for her study, and gamely we agreed. Undaunted by a severe lack of rats that year, we went out with the provided live-traps and set them despite the scarcity of sign. Impeded by ice choking the rivers, freezing swamps and an almost complete absence of muskrats, we resorted to using more effective fleece-padded leg-hold traps.

After a two-week struggle we finally caught one small rat. We found him sitting among the cattails, glowering with tiny eyes, head tilted back and jaws wide open, exposing long, small, powerful yellow teeth in a silent threat. I let Miki try to remove him from the trap.

"Ow-witch! Con-found it!" Miki snarled, shaking her heavily gloved hand after the first try. "He had trouble going through the leather, but when his teeth hit my finger they went right in!" Blood dripped readily from the wound and by that evening it had swelled up tremendously and actually remained swollen for months after the injury healed.

We finally had the rat safe in a live-trap. His foot, injured by the trap despite the padding, swelled up and he looked quite sick by evening. We left him alone with a few small potatoes, not expecting him to eat after the recent trauma.

Next day the spuds were gone, marking the beginning of a feast in which the incredible little critter just about cleaned us out. Neither pain, shock, illness nor captivity could dull his appetite. Still, he did look sick and the swelling in his foot seemed serious. Miki and I decided to try antibiotics to fight the infection. The dosage for our dogs was two pills twice a day, so an animal of Rat's size should require one-tenth of a pill twice a day.

Miki cleverly mixed the yellow powder from a capsule with ten milliliters of water and drew off one milliliter of the solution. Then we faced the problem of forcing the potion past his fierce teeth and down his chubby throat.

I let Miki try first.

Each time she bent over him, Rat threw back his head, jaws agape and teeth primed to strike with rattlesnake speed. Miki jammed the loaded syringe into the wide-open mouth and gave a short squirt. The medicine dribbled out. Rat had sucked his cheeks together so the medicine didn't even reach his tongue.

Undaunted, Miki shoved the syringe in farther and

gave another tentative squirt. Rat looked surprised. He grabbed the syringe in his little paws and tried to jerk it away. Miki recovered her grip, alarmed by his ferocity. But he was lapping up that tetracycline and chewing on the syringe. He loved the stuff! All we had to do was force a taste past his tucked-in cheeks, and he'd take over. His foot healed quickly and his appetite for potatoes and tetracycline grew to monstrous proportions.

We intended to send Rat to town on the twice-weekly mail plane, but one week the lake was too rough for the boat, the next time the plane cancelled due to bad weather, and a few days later the water pump on the outboard froze up for the winter. Meanwhile that muskrat was making a dent in root-cellared potatoes. We finally paddled him across the lake in the canoe and stuffed him onto the Cessna from Harold's Air as he glowered placidly around with his tiny, myopic eyes.

"Bye-bye, little rat," I said softly as he flew away. "And good riddance!" Finally we could turn our attention to the last major chore of freeze-up: fishing for the dogs. During the fall run of whitefish, we stake nets in the lake and freeze our catch with the coming frosts. During the winter this fish is cooked with rice, tallow and meat powder or dry dog feed.

Some days we catch fifty, eighty or a hundred whitefish in our nets, though most days yield more like thirty. A thousand fish is a good number to fill out our feed shed with, but most years we have about six hundred. The fish run starts during freeze-up when ice makes travel difficult, when outboards freeze and the last thing you want to do is sit for two hours on the aluminum canoe seat in a bitter wind, picking dozens of half-frozen fish from tangled nets while clots of snow and ice glide by toward the river mouth.

As the ice closes in, we find ourselves forcing the canoe through a mile or more of skim ice to reach the nets. Then, suddenly, we are icebound. The nets, two miles away, are in the

# PHOTOS

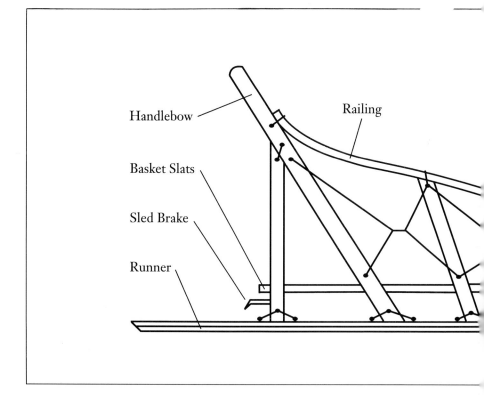

Handlebow

Railing

Basket Slats

Sled Brake

Runner

# TRAPLINE DOGSLED

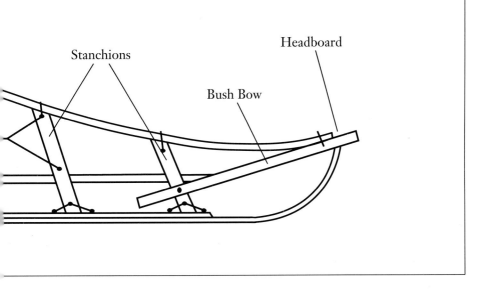

Stanchions

Headboard

Bush Bow

*Page 105:* Julie's the twin at left here, but she'll answer to Miki. Few can tell us apart and it seldom matters. The furs we're holding are red fox, which will go into fur hats we make to sell, and marten, to be sold at auction in Canada. This is only part of a winter's catch.

*Far left:* Ray could catch birds out of the air, martens in the trees, and rabbits as they sped by. He "just grabbed" this immature bald eagle, then released it unharmed. The prize was in the catching.

*Left:* Miki pricks a gas bubble on the surface of the lake ice and puts a torch to it. The escaping methane bursts into blue, white and yellow flame, blindingly beautiful against the black of the night.

*Above:* Marmee, a retired geologist, and Daddy, retired from the Federal Aviation Administration, find time to enjoy their life in the wilderness.

*Right:* Jeff Coe, Ray's buddy, builds a new cache at Birch Cabin to keep food, skins and gear safe from four-footed marauders. A metal band around the treetrunk frustrates climbing animals. Stout rungs nailed to the trunk serve as a ladder.

*Left:* Ray, at the farthest reach of our trapline, talks to Daddy at home. We could climb a nearby ridge, bounce the radio signal off Denali, and reach Fairbanks, a hundred and fifty miles to the northeast.

*Below:* Handsome black-and-white Loki was our first sled dog, and he gave us more in work, dedication and adoration than any other dog we've ever owned. Tok (right) was the most intelligent. He understood without being taught, he reasoned, and he found his own ways to communicate.

*Right:* Comet and Streak, identical twins like ourselves, were sons of Loki and Kiska. They grew alarmingly, but became two of our hardest-working dogs, full of humor, character, dedication and friendship.

*Below:* With the dogs running free, Julie grips the handlebow and takes the plunge. Seconds later, both she and sled are airborne. Visitors to Denali can see this drop-off from Eielson Visitors Center, to the west.

*Above:* Miki ferries gear across the waist-deep creek to Birch Cabin. The water, fresh from melting glaciers, is swift and cold but her pack, mostly sleeping bags, isn't heavy.

*Left:* Julie shovels the old dirt off the roof of Birch Cabin so new sheeting and fresh sod can be laid. This summer chore must be done every few years.

*Right:* Though winter may bring temperatures down to sixty below, or colder, running the fishnets at freeze-up is our coldest job. Here Miki picks the net, ice forms on the canoe, and snow builds up on the beach. But we don't have to dry these fish. They'll be stored frozen.

*Below:* Julie is hanging yarn to dry. We brush the dogs when they're shedding, wash and dry the hair, spin it into a heavy yarn and wash and dry it again, then knit it into caps for sale.

*Far right:* Julie and Pepper, our young house dog, display our biggest pumpkin. The hardier vegetables thrive here, especially the cole crops, and we grow enough each summer to last until the next harvest.

*Above:* Dogsleds get hard use on the winter trails. On-the-spot repairs are often necessary and complete overhauls are part of the summer's work. Sometimes it's better to scrap a sled and use its unbroken parts as replacements in other sleds.

*Right:* The usual catches are whitefish, pike, suckers and burbots, an occasional salmon and a rare sheefish. The lake trout in Julie's left hand, here, will go to the dinner table.

*Left:* Ray notches a log for one wall of a new Spruce Cabin to replace the third in a series that Slim Carlson had built here. We used the door from the latest old cabin and on it, caught on a bent nail, is a wisp of white hair, part of Slim's legacy to us.

*Below:* Miki leads the way as we carry fresh moss for the roof of Birch Cabin, a summer chore that needs to be done every few years. The dense, spongy moss provides living insulation.

*Right:* Miki pauses on a golden fall day, but not for long. She's heading out to bring in a load of moose meat. Then we'll harvest the potatoes and pick wild cranberries.

*Below:* All puppies are appealing. These are from a litter of ten. When they're big enough we let them run alongside the team and then, at six or eight months, we start harness-breaking them.

*Left:* Fluffy, happy Amber never got hurt nor depressed and never slacked off. In the team her tugline was always taut, and she carried a pack as if it was a part of her.

*Below:* The Collins family, with two planes and five licensed pilots, takes flying for granted. The Supercub, Julie at the controls here, gives fast, easy access to the farthest reaches of the trapline, or to Fairbanks for medical attention and shopping.

*Above:* Mail day is the big day of the week, when the neighborhood gathers to help unload the plane from Fairbanks and pick up mail and freight. It's usually the only time we get to visit.

*Right:* Breakfast on the trail to Telida. The dogs rest while we cook and eat oatmeal. One of Kiska's pups, sister of Comet and Streak, was with us for delivery to friends near McGrath.

*Left:* Julie, on the Yukon Quest, applies oinment to the dogs' feet, a chilly chore that must be done daily on the race trail to keep the skin supple and prevent infection.

*Left:* Preparations for a major race include shipping food, dog food and gear to checkpoints along the trail. Here, Miki loads part of her Iditarod shipment into the pickup. It will be flown to the checkpoints.

*Above:* We live, work and play in the shadow of the High One, Denali, 20,320 feet, tallest peak on the continent and, in rise from base to summit, one of the tallest on earth. In this view, from our front lawn in August, Denali is bathed in sunset colors under a full moon.

*Right:* Julie snowshoes toward the High One while the plucky dogs pull the sled through deep snow.

*We love our life in this land*
*and to share it would be to lose it, but*
*with stories and photos*
*we can be generous.*

river mouth and still free of ice, but we can't reach them until the lake ice is solid enough to travel on. After a couple of days, if we're lucky, we can tow a canoe to the river behind the dog team and continue checking the nets for a few more days before freeze-up is complete and the trapping season begins.

Some years we just don't catch enough fish, so we set a net under the lake ice in November. This involves a great deal of work, for the net must be threaded under the ice and the poles holding it in place must be chopped out every time we check it. Removing fish from the nets in gale winds and at temperatures down to thirty below is mighty cold business, but some years it must be done. A couple of years ago, when we'd spent too much money on the dogs, entering them in races and such, we didn't have the funds for expensive dog feeds. The day after the lake froze over we went out onto the ice.

The thin black ice bent and groaned under our weight, but it was new ice, unlike rotten ice which doesn't bend and groan but rather breaks without warning. On the young ice we moved cautiously but confidently despite the sharp cracks which ran and echoed for miles across the lake like a discordant orchestra.

Every six feet we cut a hole through the thin ice, and then pushed an eight-foot pole under the glassy surface from hole to hole. A rope tied to the end of the pole was then used to pull the sixty-foot net under the ice. It meant a lot of work, but at least cutting ten holes through one inch of October ice was far easier than cutting ten holes through November ice two feet deep.

"We'd better catch fish now," I grumbled. "With all the work it takes, I'll be real mad if we don't catch twenty or thirty fish tomorrow."

The next afternoon we pulled out the net, leaving a rope under the ice to replace it, and we found only eight fish.

With deep sighs we plunged the net back underwater and trudged toward home, moaning over our plummeting bank accounts. Miki composed a short song, the Bush Musher's Lament, and we cheered ourselves by singing it as loudly as we could while we skidded home on the glassy ice:

"You set all your nets and what do ya get
Eight lousy fish and deeper in debt
Saint Peter don't you call me 'cause I can't go
I owe my soul to Alaska Feed Co.!"

Although most years we spend late autumn fishing and gearing up for trapping, the first year after school we skipped all that and headed for the trapline as soon as our moose and potatoes were in. We anticipated spending several weeks working on the long-neglected cabin and trails. Birch Cabin was just fifteen miles away in a straight line, but to reach it by boat involved a hundred-mile trip. Daddy gave us a lift in his big riverboat the first eighty miles downriver, but then we took our canoe eighteen miles up the swift, shallow creek to the cabin. Sleet and snow flew thick as we started upriver in the last week of September. Four huskies raced around as we snaked up shallow sandbars, cut into eddies, and crept along cut banks.

The first night was snowy and damp, but all right until our puppy Mitsy chewed through the guy ropes of our improvised tarp shelter and it collapsed on us. We left early that morning and paddled steadily for twelve hours, stopping only a couple of times to eat.

At six that evening we heard a frightful roar back in the woods. The dogs had found a bull moose in rut.

I swung the canoe against the far bank and Miki grabbed the rifle from its case. The dogs came hustling when we called, apparently realizing the moose was too much to tangle with. We started cautiously on, eyes peeled and ears pricked for more trouble. Then Loki disappeared.

Another rumbling snarl sounded from the dense brush, this time in harmony with the deep bay of Loki's battle cry. I wasn't about to go smashing through that thicket after a dog tangling with a bull in rut. All we could do was grab Trapper, another lover of the chase, and keep the two females under sharp vocal control. The pandemonium across the river grew more violent and closer to the bank.

We had the canoe against the far shore and were holding our remaining dogs when three more moose burst around the curve of the river up ahead and trotted toward us, two cows and a calf, and they were coming fast. They came right down the middle of the river, their huge hooves sending great sprays of water before them as they hurtled through the two-foot-deep silt water.

Miki raised the .308 and fired into the air. I don't think the moose even heard it. She fired again. This was getting serious. The moose weren't really charging in formation, but they weren't about to stop for our paltry presence, either. Miki fired again.

"Hold you last shots!" I shouted across the booming rifle and crashing hooves. They were close enough, we might have to put one down before they stopped. The .308 holds only five shots, and the two we had left weren't really enough to do the job.

As I spoke the moose faltered and coasted to a stop twenty yards upriver. We waited. They waited. We banged on the aluminum canoe and yelled at them. They glared, especially the big cow in the lead. I didn't like her.

Miki and I glanced at each other. The moose exchanged irritated looks too, but finally the lead cow turned away and coolly walked up the bank into the trees on the far side, followed by her companions. Just then Loki came bounding up, soaked from swimming the river below us. He's usually a determined hunter, but this time he was too far from home and his prey was too big and fierce.

Paddling the heavily loaded canoe made for hard, slow work, and late rains made the river high and unseasonably fast. Instead of reaching the cabin that night we had to camp in a two-inch snowfall. In the morning we paddled through a frosty mist, and saw several more moose before the fog lifted and the animals melted back into the brush.

The damp air made our hands icy cold, but we kept on without stopping until we reached the cabin. We had paddled a total of twenty-three hours to go eighteen miles. At Birch Cabin we worked on old trails, cut wood, picked cranberries and fixed up the cabin, which had been unused for several years. A fish trap, a small weir and a gillnet in the creek all took a great deal of time to maintain as the rivers slowly froze over, but we caught only two small salmon and a misguided beaver.

That was one of those years when winter comes and goes for a couple of months before settling in. The ponds froze up, the river ice began closing in, and we'd get some snow. Then we'd get some rain, the ice would thaw, the snow melt, and we'd sit back for a few more days despite our eagerness to break out the dogsleds.

Ray was at home caring for our other dogs, and one day he told us by radio that he had to make a flight to town, leaving the dogs for a few days. Nobody in his right mind goes walking across the marshes at this time of year, but I decided to head down to tend the dogs until Ray returned.

I had eighteen miles to walk, and though a few inches of sodden snow lay on the wet ground, most of the swamps weren't frozen well. The lakes had frozen last week, but the ice had begun to rot and melt and might not be safe. I anticipated a slow trip. It was not quite seven — not quite dawn — when Miki and I slid the canoe into the silent black water slipping past

Birch Cabin. After a couple of miles on the river, I'd have to cut cross-country.

Our old malemute Trapper jumped eagerly into the canoe with us. He preferred riding to dashing through the wet brush on the bank as the current sent our canoe whipping downstream. My broad paddle drove through great clots of slush which had been drifting downstream for two weeks. Even the thaw of the last three days had not affected the river much as it sank into the curiously powerful but lethargic state just before the shelf ice closed over the current for the winter.

I left Miki and the canoe where our winter trail cut away from the river. With a light pack and the dog I set out into the tules. Hiking eighteen miles in hip boots is no easy chore, and though I was in good shape from canoeing and sawing wood, I hadn't been doing much walking. The winter trail followed open swamps most of the way, so I had to push through the spindly tamaracks alongside the long marshes.

I stopped for lunch at the halfway mark, feeling bone tired already. I ate my meat and crackers and deep-fried dough-nuts while elbowing Trapper away. He was soaking wet from falling through thin ice into the creek. The silly old dog started bawling for help, as usual, despite all his bravado when he wasn't in danger. I ended up dragging him out by the scruff, scolding him lightly for giving up so easily. Still, I was grateful for his company and he stayed close by, cheerfully following me across hip-deep marshes, over thin ice, and through dripping trees.

For all his show and pride, Trapper was simply a coward. He was beautiful and he knew it; he was powerful and he knew it; but he only *thought* he was brave. When the chips were down he'd panic. His true character shone through shortly after lunch, when we had to cross a log bridge spanning a creek. Actually it was just a pole. As I inched my way over black water ten feet deep, the pole sagged gently toward the water.

Trapper was no acrobat, but he didn't want to be left behind. He did all right until he got halfway across and then he froze, claws rigidly gripping the pole.

"Trap! Come on!" I urged. He lost his balance, panicked and made a run for it. A splendid splash marked his failure, and for the second time I grabbed his thick ruff and dragged him ashore. "Silly old boy," I told him.

We had six miles to go, and with a string of lakes ahead I hoped the walking would be more pleasant. If the ice was safe. The ice on the first lake looked thick and white, plenty strong enough for us to march across. The second showed patches of weaker black ice, but I could skirt most of them. The third lake was better, the fourth worse. Tiptoeing over the treacherous ice, I made a mental note to pick up a stout stick on the next portage. If I fell in, a stick to lean on and spread out my weight could make the difference between living and dying. But I was tired, I'd been on the trail for nine weary hours, and I forgot.

The fifth lake looked really bad. Half an inch of meltwater lay on the rotting ice, with a skim of new-formed ice on top of that. The skim ice crackled as I walked, drowning out any lower creaking that might indicate sagging ice below. I stayed near the edge, but not so close as to be on ice made weak by marsh plants.

The skim ice shivered and splashed forebodingly under my boots, and I could imagine the main ice bending under my weight. I moved faster. Then a gut instinct turned me toward shore and I hurried for safety, my feet lightly gliding over the thin ice.

With no warning I dropped into six feet of deadly black water which rushed over me, driving rods of cold through my thick wool sweater and undershirt and pouring into my tall boots as great air bubbles burst upward.

The cold knocked me breathless, but it didn't occur to

me that I might not be able to get out. I was simply annoyed, wondering whether I'd have to light a fire to warm up, or whether I could push on for the last two miles home.

With my forearm on the ice edge, I reached outward with my other hand and heaved myself upward and forward, kicking furiously, angry at the hip boots which weighed me down. One more pull and —

But the ice gave way under my weight, slowly sinking to ease me back into the water. The gut-freezing lake water swelled over me again. Oddly, my shoulders rose above the water. The light sleeping bag stuffed in my pack was acting as a buoy to hold me up.

I had to try again, with all the strength I could muster. Heaving and kicking, I burned up all my extra energy and again found myself on the brink, half in and half out, my strength gone. I stopped, panting, on the ice edge. Before I rallied, the thin ice slowly sagged, gave way, and gently but firmly thrust me back. This time the cold overwhelmed me and I gasped for air as panic rose.

I tried again. And again. And again, each time more and more aware that I might fail after all, that I might die here. If I could break my way to shore — but that was thirty feet off, and with all my energy going into each effort to roll onto the ice, I still broke only a few inches forward each time.

For a moment I rested, exhausted, fighting the cold and thinking about all the great adventures I would miss out on if I died. Then I saw Trapper sitting on the swamp grass by shore, watching me closely.

"Trappie, come!" I called faintly. He rose hesitantly, knowing why I was in trouble and knowing also the danger to himself if he obeyed me. As he faltered I realized what he already knew, that he might fall in too. And he might shove me right under as he tried to save himself.

"Stay! Stay!" I shouted as loudly as I could when he put one foot forward. "Lie down! Stay!" He sat down obediently, but he still looked worried.

My own fear was rising to a height I had never known before. The cold had begun paralyzing my limbs and I could hardly pull myself partway onto the ice, yet to break my way to shore I had to lean heavily and repeatedly on the edge of the hole. My hip boots hampered my efforts as I kicked and struggled, and each time I sagged back as the ice crumbled away.

I had used my reserve energy to struggle ten feet toward shore. How could I manage the next twenty feet? Dipping my toes into the lake and periously dropping my chin under water, I felt for the bottom. It was not there.

Finally, head down, legs limp, elbows gouging the ice edge, I started saying my prayers. A moment later I sensed something above me, something alive. Looking up, I was startled to see Trapper's anxious face over me. He had crept up unnoticed as I struggled for my life.

Even as I lifted my head, his forepaws sank into the edge of the hole. The ice was giving away.

"No! Go away!" I tried to push him back, but too late. The ice collapsed under his feet.

Gasping with horror, Trapper wheeled to flee, bolting away from that threatening black hole to save his own skin.

Action was faster than thought. As the dog snapped around my hand shot out and miraculously curled around the base of his plumy white tail. He tried to pull away, but my grip stopped him. At the same time I uttered a command, a command he knew well.

"Hike, Trapper, *hike!*"

Fear and that command lent a wondrous strength to his already powerful legs. As if he were in harness, Trapper lowered his head, belly down as his claws dug into the soft ice, and he pulled with everything he had.

With a single tremendous lunge Trapper heaved me halfway from the water, farther than ever before. When he realized I was holding him over that deathly hole he stopped, turned halfway toward me — almost as though to bite my hand to free himself — and he started sobbing.

Another command might just scare him. I eased my grip on his tail, pretending to release him. Thinking he was free, Trapper leaped for shore again. I clamped down on his tail and again roared, "Hike!"

A second huge drive forward brought me almost free of the water and I let him go. He could help me no more, and his weight combined with mine might overburden the weak ice under us. The dog scuttled ashore, leaving me to pull myself along on my belly until I was well away from the hole. Then I crawled ashore.

Dragging off my long boots, I poured two gallons of water from each one. Then I dug out a couple pieces of candy and ate them. Then I started walking. After pushing hard for a mile I felt warm enough to go on in safely. I walked around the last lake.

Trapper was tired when we arrived home, but to him it had been just another day's work. I was sore for three days. Luckily by the time I started back for Birch Cabin I felt better, and a slight freeze had hardened up the lake ice.

Trapper came along, of course, this time pulling a light hand-sled loaded with goodies for the trapline. My admiration for the dog had increased considerably. I knew the old boy was still a coward at heart, but a heroic coward.

# 8

# A FLYING FAMILY

flying is taken for granted in our family. Daddy has flown for decades, from the flatlands of Oklahoma to the mountains of the Alaska Range. Marmee earned her pilot's license before she learned to drive a car. Ray soloed at sixteen. Miki and I trailed him, but we were flying before we reached twenty.

The flying machine changed the face of Alaska and the way it developed. With no roads, the only feasible methods of travel in the old days were by foot or boat in the summer, and by snowshoe, dog team or horse-drawn sleigh in the winter. When the airplane arrived, it brought the miracle of instant transportation over a land of bogs and mountains, where traditional means of travel took weeks. Now planes are indispensable to the bush way of life. They connect village to town, they bring mail and groceries and building materials, chickens and babies and snow machines into the bush. They evacuate the sick, bring home the healed, and provide us all with a sense of security, the proof that civilization is there waiting to serve us. It's good to know it's there, even if we shudder at the thought of its coming here.

For many years Daddy flew the family around in his powerful Cessna 180, the family workhorse of the North. Marmee's Supercub on floats served us well, too, although only a two-seater. When we were very small Daddy flew the Cub while Marmee held Ray on her lap in the passenger seat, and Miki and I crammed into the small baggage compartment with the dog and plenty of goodies for an evening picnic on some uninhabited lake.

We had plenty of fun with those airplanes, even if Miki and I did get airsick on every flight. We flew up to Daddy's old cabin on the Kobuk River, we flew to Fairbanks to experience the big city, we flew to nearby rivers to search for colorful agates. As chief of the Flight Service Station, Daddy was called on occasionally to go on search and rescue missions, or to fly sick people into town for medical treatment. Each winter he flew a couple of planeloads of fish up to Slim Carlson on his trapline to save the old trapper from freighting a ton or so of dog feed fifty miles by dog team. Each fall Daddy used the plane for spotting moose to hunt, and sometimes flew a canoe tied onto the floats far upriver so he could float down and hunt on the way home.

After marriage, Marmee didn't fly so much, and as Ray earned his license and Miki and I began working on ours, the competition for the planes got too keen. But while we were very young she flew us around frequently. Once she took Daddy waterskiing behind the floatplane. She got the plane up on the step and went skimming across the lake with Daddy streaking along behind. It went fine until the plane lifted off and she didn't realize it. Daddy hadn't done much waterskiing before, and he'd already come most of the way across the lake — almost six miles — but he stuck with it, streaking along behind the flying plane at about forty miles an hour.

For a few years while we attended school, Daddy landed on a narrow, rough mud strip across the bay from home. Late one evening the Cessna 180 hit a pothole, bounced into the willows and ground-looped. The sacks of groceries in back, including eggs and peaches, were in fine shape but the plane itself suffered badly and was sold. Daddy broke out Marmee's neglected old Cessna 140, which held only two people instead of four, and after that we used the smaller Cessna and the Supercub for getting around.

Ray and Miki and I all learned to fly in that little Cessna, the same plane Marmee flew just after getting her license many years earlier. Its performance was questionable on short airstrips, though, and for trapline work we preferred the more agile Supercub.

Early one winter's day Ray took the Supercub, then on skis, out to the end of the trapline for a day's work. The temperature dropped rapidly during the day, and as dusk fell and Ray didn't return, Daddy began to grow worried. Before darkness closed in he fired up the Cessna and took off to check on his son. As he left he gave Miki and me his strongest flashlights.

"When I get back, run down to the bay and shine these lights so I can see to land," he told us. He wasn't gone very long, but night had fallen when we heard the gentle drone of the 85-horse engine. We bolted excitedly for the frozen bay, shining the lights to mark the beginning of the ski strip. A wing strut almost clipped off my head as the plane settled gently to earth, but Daddy landed safely in almost total darkness. He had seen Ray, who was all right, but Daddy didn't know why he hadn't returned. The next day at dawn we learned the rest of the story when the old red Cub came in.

Ray had spent most of the day walking in from his landing site to a cabin and back, and the plunging temperature caught him off guard. He didn't have a heater, and the cold engine wouldn't start when he was ready to head home. Undaunted by the thirty-below chill, he spent the night beside his plane, heating the engine with a fire placed to one side. He got it going, but not until after dark, so he ate some of the emergency rations stored in the baggage compartment and stuck it out until daylight. He couldn't curl up in his heavy sleeping bag because he needed it to cover the engine to keep it warm, and he spent most of the night by the fire or searching for more wood to burn. He accidentally scorched one wooden ski on the plane, but luckily nothing caught fire.

The mishap probably taught him the value of emergency gear, and also the importance of bringing along an engine heater even if you don't plan to shut down the engine for long.

Cold-weather flying — at temperatures below zero — is always a risk and we generally don't fly often during the winter unless we have a good reason to. While we were in school, Daddy flew us home frequently on warm weekends and over Christmas vacations, but all too often cold weather moved in by the time we had to get back to school and we had to fight the bitter cold back to town.

Daddy wouldn't fly when it hit forty below, but even at thirty below serious problems could come up. One very cold day we were headed back to Fairbanks when congealed oil in the engine plugged up the breather tube. Pressure built up until things blew out, and then we lost our oil and had to make a forced landing at Nenana, the only village between home and Fairbanks.

Another time Daddy and I were flying some dogs home

in the Cub when a valve broke and we lost a cylinder. The engine started running very rough, and though Daddy kept it in the air we couldn't gain the altitude we needed to cross over the mountains in our path. We made an eighty-mile detour around the mountains, wondering at every moment whether the engine might start flying apart under the stress. I spent the time hunched in the back seat, a huge cooker on my lap and two very nervous dogs drooling over my shoulder as I struggled to communicate with home on a small ham radio. The idea of making an emergency landing on the snowy hills and swamps below was extremely unappealing.

For the most part, our planes stay on the ground during the winter. The work required in getting them aloft is simply too much. The skis need to be dug out from the snowdrifts, the wings cleaned of frost and snow, a runway marked on the snowy lake, deadly cold gas filtered into the tanks, and the engine heated with a gas heater.

Even a parked plane requires some attendance. Snow must be brushed off the wings as it accumulates, so it doesn't weigh them down, and if the plane is drifted in it must be dug out before spring comes and the snow melts. One year we parked our plane out on the flats where it wouldn't drift so deeply, and a big wind damaged one wing strut. Then we moved it to a small cove where it was completely protected from the wind. Storms blew all around the cove, though, and the drifting snow settled in the hollow until the poor bird was up to its beak in snow. The eight-foot snowdrift completely buried one wing, and the job of carefully shoveling away the snow without damaging the fragile fabric-covered wings and fuselage took many days.

We almost never go to town during the winter, but in the summer, any time we make up a long grocery list we'll head to town for a day or two of shopping. Because of the expense and because it's hard to get away from our daily chores, we don't do much pleasure flying, but it's nice to get to town once a month or so during the summer.

We also use the airplane for getting out to the trapline during the summer. Although we don't trap in the summer, there's always plenty of maintenance work to be done, from repairing cabins and cutting firewood to building dog houses, caches and ladders. In late August or September we like to spend a day or so out there picking cranberries, which will keep well until winter if they are put into a cardboard box, or even a plastic bag, and cached out of reach of bears. It's also fun to hike the trails, even if they are pretty swampy, and though we don't have time for much trail work in the summer, we can locate old cubbies and traps which are hidden under the snow in the winter.

We couldn't do any of this without the airplane. The first stretch of our trapping country covers vast swamps with rivers, creeks and sloughs lacing through bogs and marshes too thin to walk on and too thick to push a boat through. A canoe can reach our Birch Cabin, but it involves a two-hundred-mile round trip and we just don't have time for that.

Instead, we skim over the swamps and bogs and willow thickets and taiga in the airplane. There's no landing place close to any of our cabins, so we choose a lake a few miles away from each place, and land there on floats. The hike in generally involves wading across a few creeks and rivers and pushing through the brush to circle deep marshes, but that's all in a day's work.

For two or three glorious days — however long we can leave the dogs in someone else's care — we bask in the golden sunlight, cool as it filters through the tall spruce, and fritter away our time picking berries, fishing for grayling and swimming briefly in the glacial river.

Our vacation speeds by too fast and we head home once again, stripping to cross a creek, walking two miles, stripping again to cross another creek, and then pushing through the forest to bypass swamps until we reach higher ground and can follow our winter trail to the lake where the float plane is parked. We always approach the plane with some trepidation, because you never know when a bear might tear into it. We've hauled so much dog food in it that removing the emergency food in back isn't going to take care of the scents wafting out to lure scavengers. So far we've been lucky; no bears have rifled or mauled the plane.

Early one fall Miki and I had spent two days in idle bliss at Birch Cabin. The hike out was wet from crossing the rivers, and hot from the sun, and we were glad to reach the tattered old Supercub where it sat tied on the lake.

"There's a little water in this tank," Miki told me as we balanced on the pontoons, giving the plane a preflight inspection.

"OK, I'll take off on the left tank. There's not much gas left in it, but it'll get us high enough so I can turn back and land if the water causes any trouble."

Miki carefully drained out all the water, which had probably leaked in during an early rain shower. Once in the air I switched tanks and we didn't have any trouble as I angled over to the Moose Pasture. Thunderheads boiled nearby, but here the air was fairly calm as I swung and looped slowly down the long pasture toward home.

We had almost reached home when the engine suddenly lost power. Not all its power, just enough to scare me spitless. It dropped down to an asthmatic idle and we started going down. I'd been flying low to spot moose, and we didn't have far to earth.

Miki sat bolt upright. "Did you do that?"

"No!" My fingers flew, switching gas tanks, pulling on the carburetor heat, working the throttle.

"I didn't think so. I just wanted to make sure."

"What should I do?" I wailed. Looking hastily around I saw two alternatives: I could try to stretch the glide to hit the bay in front of our house, or hang a sharp left and plunk down on Two Lakes, a mile from home. My instinct was to head for home. My guts told me I'd never make it.

A sharp bank brought us over the second of the two small lakes and then we were down, skimming across the sparkling blue water. Then the engine quit.

"Still alive," I said, in a trembling sweat as the plane coasted to a stop.

"Holy moly!" Miki said. "What now?"

"Dig out my radio. We'll call Daddy and ask *him* what to do!"

On Daddy's advice, which boomed in over the airways from a scant mile away, I ran up the engine and did some high-speed turns on the step. It ran fine on the right tank, but the left had run dry. That explained why it quit on the lake, but not why it had failed in the air, when it was on the right tank.

We thought the engine had choked on a bit of water, but at home Daddy drained the tank and found only good, clean gasoline. The only other likely explanation was carburetor icing, which can occur on a warm, humid afternoon if the pilot isn't watchful. Usually a light drop in power signals the onset of icing, but in circling to look for moose I had been constantly adjusting the throttle and any change in power probably went unnoticed.

The episode left me a little shaken and grateful for the luck of having a suitable emergency landing site within range. Miki brushed the whole thing off cheerfully and composed the Bush Pilot's Prayer:

"Now I take me off to fly
I pray the Lord I do not die
But if I crash before I land
I hope to God the explosion's grand!"

My flying career actually got off the ground as the result of a much more serious flying accident. While we were going to school in Fairbanks we knew we needed to fly ourselves, instead of depending upon Daddy and Ray all the time. We had already completed ground school, but an aversion to all things mechanical stood in the way of actual flying lessons.

In 1978 we three kids spent Christmas at home alone, as our parents were on a trip. Actually, Miki and I were at home and Ray and his buddy, Jeff Coe, were in and out. Much of the time they spent at Grayling Creek at the end of Slim's trapline, commuting by ski plane each time they needed food or a well-earned break from life in a windowless cabin smaller than a wall tent. Marten swarmed the hills that year, and the two were jubilant with their catch.

Jeff was an easy-going guy, tall, blond, blue-eyed, a contrast with Ray, who was shorter and broader, with brown hair and hazel eyes, and always spoiling to "do good quick." Both were pilots, Ray more confident, Jeff more careful. Because the Supercub belonged to us, Ray did the flying on the trapline, but when we headed back to town Jeff flew his little Cessna 140 with Miki and our cat. Ray and I, with a big bundle of furs, our little house dog, Pingo, and a pair of skis wedged against the door, packed ourselves into the Cub.

The orange and white Cessna skimmed off the drifted lake first, and then Ray hit the throttle and the Cub roared forward. Ray took off straight across the bay instead of down the length of it, so in seconds we were floating over willows on the far side. Then the engine quit.

"Oh-oh —" Ray said under his breath. His hand shot

out to switch gas tanks, and immediately the 135-horse engine roared mercifully in our ears. We regained a little altitude, circled, and landed to determine the trouble.

Ray ran up the engine and gave it a thorough check. It ran smoothly on both tanks and he deduced (he always deduces) that a temporary air lock in the line, made by a nearly empty gas tank, had caused the failure. I didn't question his judgment; I didn't know anything about it.

Again the broad-winged craft soared gracefully skyward, climbing effortlessly in the smooth air while the fuselage reverberated with controlled power. I snuggled my face against warm, black little Pingo, thinking how good it would be to eat at a restaurant and take a long bath after a month of moose meat and snow water.

Then the engine quit again. We were hardly three hundred feet above the snow-covered lake.

Ray set the plane in a gentle bank. We don't know why; he doesn't remember. Perhaps to avoid rough drifts or an open channel of water below us. Meantime Jeff, missing us, had circled back and passed overhead just as we glided toward earth. Maybe it was a bit of turbulence from his higher airplane, or more likely a wind shear next to the nearby hill, but some sudden rough air set our powerless plane almost on its right side.

Ray made a soft noise in his throat as he swiftly balanced the light plane with the controls, but too late. The high wing stalled and in an instant we flipped over onto the left side, nosed down, and headed for disaster.

Out of control, the plane spun wildly toward the ground. Jeff told me later it looked like a crash scene from a silent World War II movie. Ray told me he remembered looking forward out the windshield and seeing the white ground spinning straight ahead of him.

"Hang on, Julie!" he shouted.

He said I replied, "OK."

Miki said when we hit the ground, a plume of snow exploded like a great cloud.

I don't remember. I don't remember any of that. The impact of the crash knocked the memory out of me, and it never returned. All I remember is the initial stall.

From above, it looked as if Ray had been killed — the engine had been smashed back into the cockpit — and Miki doubted whether I had survived without serious injuries. Jeff tried to land near the wreck, but rough drifts forced him to circle and land in the smooth bay and taxi over.

The Cub's right wing had been torn nearly off. Ray lay leaning out the right door with the engine in his lap, and gasoline spilling from the ruptured left tank onto his parka. He had a fractured femur and ankle, a smashed elbow, broken teeth, a dislocated shoulder and chemical burns from the gas, but he was alive.

The front seat had collapsed on my right foot and the lightweight tubing-and-plexiglass ceiling was crumpled over my head, pinning me in the back seat with Pingo. Except for some bumps and bruises, my crushed foot and a concussion, I wasn't seriously hurt. I just didn't know what the heck was going on, nor why I was squished in here.

"You OK? You OK?" Jeff called, struggling over the wreckage. In vain he and Miki tried to extricate us. Jeff pulled an old black hanky from his pocket and stretched his long arm through the wreckage to wipe my bloody face. I waved him off, not realizing my face was injured.

After a futile effort to rescue us, Jeff left Miki to bundle us against the cold as best she could while he flew across the lake for help. He landed at Fran and Bill Holmes' place. They had run the community power plant there for three decades and had the only telephone on the lake.

Jeff skidded the Cessna right up to the shore and leaped out, hurtling our enraged cat into the depths of the plane when she tried to escape. He recruited help, phoned his parents to get assistance from Fairbanks, and charged back across the lake with Bill's hired man, Dave Galletly. His quick action went a long way toward saving us. Miki was impressed.

"I kept thinking, oh my gosh, we have to get you out of the airplane by ourselves and make three trips in Jeff's plane to get us all into town, and with Ray so dinged up I didn't know *how* we could do it!" Her reaction reflected our upbringing in the bush: it never occurred to her that we might seek help, we were so used to the isolation. Jeff was more of a town boy, and his first reaction was to seek help.

For two hours Jeff and Dave hacked away at the wreckage, sawing through tubing and pulling apart the wing and fuselage to reach Ray. Setting him gently in a snow-machine sled, they whisked him off to the house and carried the whole sled inside, setting it beside the still-warm wood stove.

I lay on the snow beside the remains of the airplane which Marmee had flown across the continent. I thought how blue the sky looked, how white the snow. I felt too weak to move, as if I might faint if I tried. Still, I picked up my head a little and peeked at the plane. I could see only the twisted tail angled rakishly toward the ground. If I tried a little harder I might see the rest of the wreck, but I decided I didn't really want to see it.

The snow machine roared back and Miki leaped off. "You OK?" she cried.

"Never been better," I replied. It took all my strength. I almost didn't make it to the house on the back of the snow machine. With an arm slung over Jeff's shoulder, I hopped into the house and collapsed on the sofa. My right foot felt totally senseless, though I didn't think it was frozen.

Miki walked back to the house, carrying Kitty while

Pingo hobbled along behind. The old dog kept stopping, but Miki couldn't carry her and the cat *both*. Finally she turned to Pingo, calling her by the pet name we had invented when she was a puppy and we were just nine years old. "Ferdeebee, you *have* to." Pingo understood and made it all the way home, although later we found she had a broken pelvis.

Once home, Miki tended us as best she could while we waited for an Army helicopter to medivac us to Fairbanks. I grabbed her once as she passed me and hissed, "I was in a plane crash!"

"I know!" she replied, her voice full of awe.

"I can't believe it! I mean, I sort of expected to be in a crash someday, but not *today*!" I was more excited than horrified. In fact, by the time the physical shock wore off late that night, the emotional shock was gone too and I felt more proud than dismayed by the adventure.

A huge Army helicopter landed in front of the cabin that evening while a big Hercules aircraft circled overhead, waiting to refuel the chopper in flight once we got under way. It was very dark by then but the night reverberated from the loud engine and rotary blades. The medic let us all aboard, even Kitty and Pingo. Only Jeff stayed behind to bring his own plane in the following morning.

I wasn't in an airplane again until spring. I didn't expect to be afraid, but I was. The moment the wheels left the ground a sudden panic hit me hard. I was all right once we gained altitude, and after a few more flights the fear subsided, but I realized I had to take control. I needed a pilot's license. Miki followed my lead, and we found an instructor. The first few lessons, six months after the crash, were filled with anxious moments, but skill and confidence ran hand in hand. By the age of twenty we had our private pilot's licenses. About the same time we bought another rickety old Supercub, so things were almost back to normal.

But not quite. Ray spent two months in a hospital, two more months in a wheelchair, and another year on crutches. I escaped with a weak foot. It doesn't stop me from doing whatever I want to do, but each day as I walk or ski or drive the dogs, a gentle ache constantly reminds me that I must not abuse my body too much, lest it wear out before its time.

# 9

# DOGS

Our life revolves around the dogs. They provide a means of transportation and a way of life. Not just because they are invaluable on the trapline, easily moving us and our gear where snow machines can pass only with difficulty, but because Julie and I have a passion for dogs. Spring, summer, fall and winter our activities center around the huskies. We strive to breed and buy the dogs best suited for this heavy work, but character and appearance often override the qualities usually touted for modern sled dogs — speed, endurance and good feet. I won't keep a bad dog, but I'm happier selling one I just don't like than losing some character who may not be the ideal sled dog but is a joy to have around anyway.

Our first husky joined our family when we were fifteen and spending winters in Fairbanks. Ray began to build a small team for use on the trapline, and that first bunch was a mis-matched crew from friends and the free-ads, consisting of three Siberians and two malemutes. I don't care much for the pure breeds, but they didn't cost us anything and at least they pulled. Two went on to become good leaders. Ray took his little team home to trap for a year, leaving Julie and me in Fairbanks for one more year of high school. We decided we could not possibly survive with only Pingo, the family pet. A friend had a friend who had taken in a stray husky and needed to find it a home. We rushed over to see it.

"He looks kind of scrawny," I said doubtfully as we stood looking at the black and white husky cowering in the yellowing September grass. At fifty-five pounds he was all skin and bones and we wanted bigger dogs, preferably seventy- to eighty-pound, long-legged, old-time trapline dogs.

"Well, let's give him a try," Julie said with all the optimism of a seventeen-year-old novice musher.

Loki, we called him, after the legendary Norse char-acter, half noble god, half clever, wicked giant, and well did he live up to his name. Looking back on the eleven years he's been with us, I have to say he has given us more than any other dog we've ever owned — more work, more lessons, more fights, more adoration, more character, more charisma, more hateful habits, more power, more dedication. His power, his dominating attitude, and direct, peculiar gaze from a lowered head convinced us he has some wolf blood in him. With his handsome black and white markings, set off by odd black spots where they shouldn't be, and a bold white blaze on his neck, he cut quite a dashing figure by the time he reached full adulthood two years later.

But as he crouched on the car floor during the drive back to the house, we realized he'd be a challenge right from the start. Somewhere, sometime, the young dog had been brutalized. He cowered at a glance, crouched when approached, and trembled at the lightest caress. For days on end we spent our free time working with him, sitting on his doghouse, talking to him, patting him. Gradually he came to accept us and finally to express gratitude for the attention we lavished upon him. He slunk from his doghouse to greet us and unbuttoned his legs so we could scratch his belly. If we were slow with a pat, he'd lift one snowy-white forepaw out to us with beseeching adoration.

During that fall before the snow fell, we walked him on a leash, practically making a pet of him. We didn't dare turn him loose no matter how hard he tugged, for fear of not catching him again. But one golden afternoon we just couldn't stand it. Walking down an abandoned, leaf-covered road, Julie reached down and slipped off the rope.

"OK, Loki!" she said, giving him a light thump on the shoulder.

At first he didn't realize he was free. He trotted ahead slightly, paused, and glanced back questioningly.

"Go on, Loki!"

He whirled away then, running fast, the sunlight rippling across his glossy coat. He never looked back, he just ran, straight away down the road, around the corner and out of sight.

Julie looked at me. I looked at Julie. What if he didn't stop?

Rounding a corner, we spied him leaping joyously after a red squirrel, darting through the trees with breathtaking grace. Then he whirled back to us, his melting amber eyes glowing. The last barrier had been broken. He was no longer an abused castaway, a prisoner of the chain and leash. He now recognized them for what they were: restraint, not imprisonment. For an instant he danced before us, then he was gone again, dashing down the road, stretching his long young limbs in fluid strides.

We walked on, and after a few minutes Julie called him to us. Instantly the light in his eyes snuffed out. The vibrant movements froze into a half-crouch. He eyed us warily.

"Loki," Julie said. "Come." He slunk toward us a few steps, head lowered, ready to dodge away. We didn't move.

"Come."

He crept closer, subdued and trembling. By the time he reached us he was practically on his belly. But he came. He came all the way to us, miserable with the thought of the restrictive leash. We knelt by him, patting and praising him, feeling the quiver under every touch. Then I stood up.

"OK, Loki!"

He gazed at me with burning yellow eyes. The leash still hung coiled in Julie's hand. For a moment he didn't understand. Then he leaped around us, the joy flooding his expressive face. He realized that we trusted him, and he was free, free not only from the leash but from the burdens of anxiety and self-doubt and mistrust. Never again would he be the cowering stray. His wild shyness remained for years, but in that simple gesture of trust we gave him a self-confidence that never let him down.

From a scrawny half-grown pup he developed into a powerful, hard-working sled dog. His eyes, the color of melting spruce pitch, mirrored the power in his spirit, sparking with a special quality not seen in many dogs, a quality of self-esteem and dedication, and sometimes, when he was looking at me, of love.

For several years we ran him as a team dog and in swing just behind the leader. He pulled hard, listened and learned, and didn't cause any trouble until he was four. Then he started to fight.

Most dogs, if they fight, will do so when they are young and trying to establish a strong position with their peers. Loki, slow to mature in mind and body, did not start until he knew all the ropes, but once started he quickly became a fearsome combatant.

Loki did not fight for fun: he fought for dominance. Every battle was a struggle for supremacy, and by the time old age brought his pugilistic career to a dwindling close, he'd chewed up nearly every male dog we ever owned. One dog, nervous and not always a good worker, seemed to Loki to be a liability to the pack — *his* pack — and he did not just fight with the poor fellow, he tried to kill him, not once but several times, and only separation prevented him. Only two dogs escaped his assaults. Yukon, a hundred-pound malemute, was afraid of him and Loki knew it, and reasoned rightly that he had no need to prove his authority in an uncertain battle. Thor, an even bigger Mackenzie River husky who arbitrarily attacked any dog he could sink his teeth into, was the only dog Loki feared, but rather than admit it he simply avoided the big husky with majestic dignity or a characteristic sneer.

His worst fighting foe was another malemute. Trapper outweighed him by ten pounds and possessed vast fighting experience, but when the time came, Loki took Trapper on without hesitation.

We were fishing for pike in a small creek downriver. The two dogs, along for the ride, had already been in one small squabble which we broke apart before either could establish himself. Trapper hovered near me, as usual. Loki trotted in sharp half-circles around us, eyeing the bigger dog wickedly, ready for an attack. The instant I turned my back the fight was on.

The two piled into a snarling, raging tangle, both young and strong with driving power. Julie leaped over and grabbed Loki by the rump, out of reach of the flashing teeth, and I seized Trapper, and with a unified heave we pitched the savage pair into the deep waters of Spencer Creek.

Trapper hit first and sank beneath the murky water. He was on his way up again when Loki struck. Even before Trapper's head had emerged, Loki literally dived under the water and drove the malemute farther down. Both dogs disappeared under the frothing bubbles as Julie and I stared in astonishment.

I was ready to go in after them when Loki finally popped up and swam slowly ashore, climbed out, and gave his dripping coat a triumphant shake. Eventually Trapper too bobbed up and dragged himself out, a humbled dog.

That fight unfortunately did not settle the matter, and for several years the two waged a war for dominance. Then, during the fall we spent at the Birch Cabin, the two had it out once and for all. Julie and I were gone for the day, leaving the dogs, including one in season, tied outside the cabin.

Trapper apparently broke his chain and went after the female. Loki, who in desperation could break any snap, link, chain or collar we ever put on him, wasted no time in making an attack. We found them in the late afternoon, chains tangled, lying in a bloody, bedraggled heap. Trapper was so weak he could hardly lift his head and we thought he was a goner. Loki fared little better, but as usual he came out a scarred winner, this time with a broken nose and fragmented teeth.

We pulled one dislocated tooth with a pair of pliers. He let us treat him as he always did, with only the softest of whines to let us know when he thought we'd hurt him more than altogether necessary.

"All done," I sang, when the offending tooth fell to the floor. He knew what that meant and instantly retreated under the table. He didn't come out for a long time, either.

That fight ended Trapper's feuding tendencies. Already an old dog, he survived and recovered more fully than Loki, but he was soon retired to a life of ease. The break in Loki's nose became a dip and that apparently messed up his airway, for he lost some of his stamina and became prone to a cough. But his career was far from over. About this time we moved him up into the lead, and over the years he proved himself one of the best leaders we ever ran. He couldn't be beaten for sheer determination, and with his fierce will he forced every dog in the team to do what he wanted. He assaulted every problem with aggression and intelligence. If he came to a bad spot of overflow he'd look back for advice. At my command he'd charge through snow up to his back, dragging the team around the hazard, or if I ordered "Straight on!" straight on he'd go, through any obstacle. He once charged shoulder-deep into a flooding creek at Julie's command, dragging seven panicky dogs in his wake, and would have swum them clear across but she thought better of it and called him back.

His experience proved invaluable. I could run him out to the wood lot the first time for the year, and he'd go to a pile of wood and turn the team around and stop without a word from me. It wasn't always the right pile. We had some serious arguments at times about what we were to do, and I didn't always come out on top. He could also judge certain hazards, especially water or dangerous ice, better from his position in the lead than I, and at times he'd override my decision and pick a safer route. Even when running back in the team, he'd get angry if a young leader took a wrong turn.

We once bred him to an eighty-pound malemute and the two pups we kept grew to weigh nearly a hundred and twenty pounds apiece. Loki took pains to keep the pair in line, and even when they outweighed him by forty pounds he'd pounce on them unawares and throw them to the ground. He lost his big canine teeth in some fight or other, and he learned to throw a dog and get out fast instead of actually fighting. This always disconcerted his opponent, while leaving Loki unscathed.

But as age took its toll the other dogs began to retaliate,

and one day three ganged up on the old leader. The fight didn't last long; Julie and I broke it right up. But we let Loki run loose the last fifteen miles to the cabin, and that evening Julie found a three-cornered gash hidden in the fur of one shoulder, four inches long and gaping open two inches to expose an impressive patch of stringy red muscles.

We were out on the trapline, with the nearest vet more than a hundred and fifty miles away by airplane, not to mention the twenty-four-mile dog-team trip to the airstrip and the five-day wait for the mail plane. Grimly I dug out the first-aid kit.

Dental floss and a fur needle had to suffice. I boiled them in a half-hearted attempt at sterilization, and we cut away all the surrounding fur we could with Julie's sharp little pocket-knife. We washed the gash with warm water and dish soap as Loki crouched on the floor. The cabin hadn't warmed up yet and trickles of blood and water froze on his dark fur. After scrubbing the wound I lifted the flap of skin and dumped in a tablespoon of Furacin antibiotic powder.

"Easy, Loki. Stay." Julie gripped him as I took the first stitch, holding the needle with a pair of pliers to force it through the tough skin. I quickly tied a few square knots, cut the thread, and took another stitch, pinning down the flap and then closing the rest of the wound evenly.

Loki whined softly when I took an extra deep stitch and I paused to pat him. "Silly old boy," I whispered, always impressed by his self-restraint and that undying faith that we were at least trying to help him.

Eight or nine stitches finished the job. "All done, Loki," I said, gently wiping the wound dry. How well he knew those words! The wound was undoubtedly contaminated, and we only hoped oral antibiotics could prevent a frightful infection.

He was pretty sick for a few days, and he spent the nights on burlap sacks near the stove. But in a couple of weeks we took the stitches out and not long after that he was back in harness. Then the wound, nearly healed, developed an abscess which swelled to the size of a small orange, and once again we were compelled to put him back on the "operating table." With a razor blade and the hole punch on Julie's knife I pierced the thick skin, and clear reddish fluid drained away. We were pleased to see no sign of infection, just an accumulation of bloody serum. The abscess drained for days, but in the end healed without so much as a white hair to mark the spot.

Loki was not our only good leader then. Of all the huskies we've kept, Tok had to be the smartest. Sled dogs are not renowned for their intelligence, but Tok proved the exception. His understanding of the English language was phenomenal for a dog who was never taught anything beyond the words *hike* and *whoa*. Yet he was so quiet and reserved, we'd had him for two years before we noticed his ability.

I discovered he could gee and haw perfectly when I was skijoring with him and one other dog, and over the years he proved to be the best gee-haw dog I ever worked. I could be breaking trail at a fast trot up a strange, unmarked swamp and any time he felt uncertain about my intended direction, he'd glance back over his shoulder.

"Gee, Tok," I'd say, and he'd swing off to the right. I never said it twice, and he never got it wrong.

Yet it was in the summer that we really noticed his sharp reasoning ability. "He *talks*," Julie insisted. He recognized the language barrier and found ways to overcome it. To attract our attention he sat and watched us with his wide, dark eyes and wiggled his ears, first one and then the other. If that didn't work, he would move sharply, catching an eye, and then sit and wiggle his ears.

"What 'cha want, Tok?" I'd ask. "You want water?" If that was it he'd stand up, lift one forepaw and bounce slightly in a most dignified manner. Sure enough, I'd check his water can and find it dry. If that wasn't the problem he'd just sit and wiggle his ears or maybe toss his nose a little until I guessed right.

In the hot summer months when the black flies drove the dogs mad, Tok would slip his collar and come looking for us in the yard where Julie and I were hanging a new fish net.

"Tok!" I scolded. "Shame on you. Go back right now." And he would. A sheepish expression on his face, tawny golden-brown tail fanning, he would turn and trot down the trail to the dog yard. I always followed and found him waiting at his chain. After this happened a few times he tired of it and dug holes in the garden instead of seeking us out.

Sometimes when the flies became unbearable, we let him inside Slim's cabin where he could relax in the cool, dark interior. Tok loved this, and even after the bugs died down he begged to go inside. Instead of running the two miles down the beach when we checked the fish nets, he'd push the door open and spend the time sleeping inside. We would lock the double doors to keep him out when we left, latching the inside door with a hook and eye and swinging the swivel block bolt across the outside door.

Twice I accused Julie of forgetting this when I returned to find Tok inside. The third time I barred both doors myself. When we returned Tok was again snoozing happily under the table, both doors standing open.

He never fought unless attacked. He simply avoided eye contact when another dog was looking for a scrap. He just pretended he didn't realize he was being challenged, and the aggressor always seemed embarrassed. The other dogs usually let him alone, especially after the slow dignity of old age caught up with him. At eleven Tok was still in harness, although weaker and hurting from arthritis. Most of the dogs had a good deal of respect for him. Thor, the 110-pound Mackenzie River husky, was the exception. Thor pulled just behind Tok in the team, and several times had charged forward and grabbed the old dog in his huge jaws in total disregard for dogfighting etiquette.

Tok was a patient dog, but Thor carried things too far. Tok didn't exactly lose his temper, but he did decide this was simply unacceptable.

When Thor leaped snarling on Tok's back I quickly stopped the team and ran forward. As I hauled back on the Mackenzie's harness, trying to get him off without being bitten myself, Tok whirled, twisted out of Thor's grip, grabbed the bigger dog by the nose, and threw him to the ground like a martial arts expert practicing on a novice.

A week later Thor attacked Tok again, savagely driving at the old dog with his powerfully huge, young body. This time I did not rush to Tok's rescue. No. I stepped back and roared, "You tell 'im, Tok!"

And he did.

On a cold December day the malemute Kiska gave birth to pups by Loki on the floor of the Birch Cabin. Although a welcomed event, the little buggers caused some problems since we were always traveling back and forth on the trapline. When they were only twelve days old we headed home for Christmas, and they took their first sled ride.

I eased my legs into the sleeping bag in the sled basket and Julie handed me the three fat black-and-white pups. Settling them in my lap, I glanced over my shoulder at my partner as she stood ready on the sled runners.

"I *don't* want to tip over," I reminded her. The corner at the bottom of the bank could be tricky with the dogs at full speed and a load in the sled.

"Oh, *nonsense!*" Julie laughed. She had no intention of dumping the sled, not with that  precious load of pups. Kiska poked her nose into the sleeping bag and I let her sniff her pups. Satisfied, she turned to her place behind the sled.

"Hike!"

The dogs responded instantly to Julie's command and the sled careened forward, narrowly missing trees on either side of the trail. Down the bank they rushed, breaking into a hard run as they hit the river.

The sled snapped around the corner and one edge of the runner caught in the hard trail. Julie struggled to keep it under control, but too late! The sled performed a splendid airborne roll, depositing me with the squeaking, squirming puppies in the snow.

Finding I had not squashed a puppy or two, I reloaded the sleeping bag, myself and the pups, and grumbled to Julie, "*Sure* we won't tip over. *Tell* me about it!"

"Hike!"

Again the team shot forward. In twenty feet the sled was zooming along in fine style, traveling nearly fifteen miles an hour, when the towrope cunningly snagged a piece of driftwood frozen in the ice.

The dogs hit their harnesses hard as the sled banged to a halt. Unfortunately I did not stop. Sleeping bag, puppies and all slid down the slippery sled basket, over the bush bow, and plop! into the snow.

I glared straight ahead. This wasn't going to be a restful ride, after all.

Despite my misgivings the rest of the trip passed without any major calamities. Oh, a tree-full of snow did avalanche down into the sleeping bag, my parka and shirt, and we did break the handlebow of the sled, but we reached home in fairly good time and duly installed the puppies in the house. This was our first litter and we guarded the infants with jealous zeal.

Over the next two weeks the three puppies grew at an amazing rate. By early January we had to move them all back to the Birch Cabin. At four weeks the pups weighed more than ten pounds each, and were toddling instead of crawling.

"We'll have to put them in a box this time," Julie announced.

"You'd better make it a *big* box," I replied drily.

She did. She found the biggest cardboard box we had, and stuffed in plenty of towels and a pair of overalls to keep the little guys warm. Then in went the pups, crawling over one another and squawking indignantly as we tied the load securely into the sled.

Julie skijored behind as I drove the nine-dog team out the trail at a good clip. After half a mile I saw with dismay a fat little black and white head poking out between the cardboard flaps. No, no! Another head popped up. The first one squeezed out farther, straining every little puppy muscle, and managed to pry out two front feet.

A third nose poked up determinedly. The first puppy renewed his efforts and scrambled most of the way out, teetering precariously over the side of the box. Visions of squishing him with a sideswiping tree flashed through my mind, and I stopped the team.

"We've got to do *something*!" I exclaimed. I snatched the overalls and the padding out to make more room, and stuffed the little travelers back in despite their vehement protests. There. I held the three bobbing heads down while Julie tied the top shut, enforcing the string with some wire she found in the handlebow bag.

"There! They'll never get out of that," Julie said, standing back to survey her work.

Half a mile farther, one puppy was sitting above the bush bow, one was about to topple over the sled railing, and the third was hanging out of the box by his hind legs.

This time we unloaded the bag of dog food from the

back of the sled — leaving it sitting in the snow where any fox or wolverine could tear into it — thus creating a hollow where the pups could sit in the sleeping bag. I left the bag open in front so they wouldn't get too hot, and, tired out from their efforts, they finally drifted into a contented slumber.

Not for long. Soon I had my hands full trying to steer the eight-foot sled, unbalanced since we'd removed the dog food. The wind-drifted trail slanted so the sled kept sliding off one side, and the pups were forever crawling out. After two dog-fights, tipping over more than once and running off the trail countless times while I struggled with the pups, my temper was ready to explode. Finally wisdom broke through rage and I stopped and jury-rigged a gee pole.

With Julie skiing on the gee pole between sled and team, she could easily steer the sled, freeing my hands to control the wee beasties in the basket. We stopped twice to let them run around in the snow, which tired them out so they slept awhile. After a long, trying trip we reached the cabin, tired to the bone and cross after a hard day with three bad dogfights. The puppies, naturally, were in fine fettle and delighted to be back.

When we headed home again on a mid-January day the wind was howling through the trees and the temperature hung at twenty below. The dogs, tired from a hard trip farther out the line, stood in glum silence as we harnessed them. I drove, with the pups buried in the sleeping bag and Julie skijoring behind the sled while Kiska ran loose. For the first four miles the trees protected us from the brunt of the blow, but when we came out onto a mile-long lake the wind was screaming unimpeded at forty miles an hour.

Halfway across we stopped to check Kiska and found her underparts were freezing. Julie melted off the ice with her bare hands, her fingers turning a brilliant red in the bitter cold as the wind whipped the drifting snow around us.

I tied a heavy wool shirt around Kiska's belly while the dogs waited impatiently, eager to escape the wind. Turning back to the sled, I had just laid hold of the handlebow when the dogs took off without warning. Instinctively I tightened my grip as they jerked me off my feet.

My sudden weight on the side of the bow pulled the sled up on edge and it crashed over, catapulting puppies far and wide. The three little bundles of fur went rolling around on the hard drifts, the piercing wind whipping snow crystals into their fuzzy coats.

I snatched up one, righted the sled, stuffed him in, and scooped up a second, my hands and wrists nearly freezing. As I shoved them deeper into the bag I spied the female, the pluckiest pup, heading bravely away across the drifts, bent on getting out of the mess on her own. I leaped after her, roaring at the dogs to *stay*! and finally crammed her into the bag with her brothers.

I ran behind the sled the rest of the way across the lake while the dogs pulled hard, as eager to get out of the wind as I was. I stopped in the lee of a few scraggly spruce at the edge of the lake. We stuffed Kiska into the bag with her puppies, and a couple of good swats persuaded her to stay put as the sled jerked forward once more.

What a long trip! The screaming wind slowed the team's speed and drained their already sagging spirits. The hardest part proved to be the last half-mile where the wind roared across open flats and lake ice. By now the gusts were hitting fifty miles an hour and the blowing snow cut visibility as much as the early darkness. Hunched on the runners to lessen the wind resistance, I shouted encouragement to the dogs at the top of my lungs, not even sure whether Loki in the lead could hear me.

"Come on, you guys, keep it up! Almost home, Loki, home, Loki! Let's go! *Good* lads!"

Each furry head bent forward, the powerful shoulders driving steadily against the whipping wind. The drag from the gale clutched and gripped at the sled, but as we crossed the bay I could see the power of that team as they pulled steadily for home, Loki with his head turned sidewise to listen for my voice.

And bless their little buttons, those puppies slept through it all. Once in the yard, we rushed them and their mother inside before unhooking the team, giving each weary dog a warm hug for a job well done, and lighting the dog-pot fire for an extra fine dinner of fish, rice and tallow. Then back to the house for our own good supper of moose stew and hot biscuits.

All that running around didn't seem to hurt the pups a bit. We kept the two males, who continued to grow at a horrifying rate, hitting fifty pounds by three and a half months. At nine months they passed the hundred-pound mark. Loki weighed about eighty pounds and the malemute mother, Kiska, was about the same.

Now I like big dogs, but not *that* big. A long-legged seventy-pound husky can travel fast enough to cover eighty miles in a day, and is powerful enough to haul a heavy load through deep, powdery snow. You don't need sixteen of them to get anywhere. But in my experience the dogs over eighty-five or ninety pounds can't often match that pace. So when Comet and Streak defied the Law of Genetics and shot past a hundred pounds, Julie and I began to worry. That was October. We didn't have to wait long to see whether they would work.

We hooked up Streak in the wheel position in a small team for the first run of the year. He was a natural. He lunged into his harness at the word "Hike!" and during the four-mile run his only mistake was to pass on the wrong side of a tree and get slammed by his neckline.

Comet didn't fare so well. Confused by the tangle of restraining lines and yowling, wildly excited dogs, he slammed on the brakes. Now, when one of your little forty-five-pound racing pups starts to drag, usually the team can pull him along until he realizes how much more fun it is to pull forward instead of backward. But when a hundred-pound puppy stops, everything stops.

Ordinarily we don't run two green pups side by side, as they tend to play and pick up bad habits from each other. But Streak had done so well we made an exception. He and Comet adored each other, and with their handsome identical black and white masks, they looked truly impressive side by side in the wheel.

It worked. When Comet saw his brother hit the harness he did the same. After that they acted like pros instead of overgrown pups, except they were so powerful we couldn't stop them even in a very small team. Once, when we'd tried everything to get them stopped, I rode the sled brake with both feet while Julie ran up, took a flying leap, and made a most professional football style tackle. She knocked both pups flat, stopping the team abruptly.

Those two pups once broke loose and trotted off across the snow dragging an ice-clad canoe loaded with whitefish that Julie and I couldn't drag three feet. Several years later, when maturity and obedience replaced puppy enthusiasm and uncontrollable power, both dogs learned to stop on command and many times I've seen them bring a big team to a halt when the other dogs were bent on running away and leaving the musher racing frantically behind.

Broken lines became the rule for our two big wheelers. Quarter-inch tuglines and necklines snapped like thread if the dogs hit a tree and jerked to a stop. Even the half-inch doubled sled harness snapped out. We bought special snaps for their tuglines because the regular 5/8-inch brass swivel snaps kept disintegrating under their power.

Our biggest concern did not materialize. Comet and Streak not only kept pace with our team, they were among the hardest, most consistent workers. Even at a dead run those hundred-and-twenty-pound dogs kept their lines tight. During his first year in harness, we put more miles on Comet than any other dog on the team because he was always up and screaming to go, even when the older dogs didn't want to come out of their houses. When they were fifteen months old, Julie and I took them on a two-week trip of nearly six hundred miles. With only five dogs in harness — plus Loki running loose with a foot injured in a dogfight the second day out — the pups outshone all but one of the adults. By the end of their first season in harness, at seventeen months of age, Comet and Streak had twenty-five hundred miles behind them.

In later years as our team's speed increased, they did not do quite so well, and on the long-distance trips and especially the long-distance races, they simply could not recover so fast as smaller dogs. They still pulled their big hearts out, but it was hard on them.

On one long, hard run during a particularly tough trip, Comet sprained his leg badly. The wrist swelled up to twice its already impressive size, and he could not put a bit of weight on it.

I could not carry him in the sled. We were fighting a bitter headwind in temperatures well below zero, and the sled was dragging so hard I was walking most of the way. I turned Comet loose to hobble along behind as best he could on three legs.

We traveled for perhaps eight hours, straight through. Comet began falling behind during the last three hours, his face set in painful determination. I could not stop; we had to get in. Whenever the other dogs became too tired I paused long enough to go hold Comet, and he never faltered, but we were still several miles out when he began wearing out. He strained every muscle, but plowing through the drifts on three legs for twenty-five miles just took everything out of him.

I saw he had fallen way back and was staggering through the drifts, holding the injured leg aloft. "Comet, Comet," I called. I had called him so often he just couldn't respond any more. Then I started to sing. I had a special song for him.

"Kamma-kamma-kamma-kamma-kamma chameleon, red-gold and green, red-gold and gre-e-en!" His ears came up. He heaved himself forward, picking up speed.

I didn't know the words right, but I sang strongly anyway.

"Kamma-kamma-kamma-kamma-kamma chameleon, he can't be seen, he can't be seen!"

He plunged forward, not fast but fast enough to overtake the team. I could have cried. He was hurting badly. He stayed with me the rest of the way in. Any time he started falling back I sang his song, and he put everything he had and more into catching up again.

We were all exhausted when we reached shelter. I went to Comet and slipped my arms around him as he sagged against me, windblown snow penetrating deep into his heavy black coat.

"Kamma-chameleon," I whispered, and I knew from the way he looked at me that he loved me in spite of it all.

I've been in some tight spots with those dogs, but they hardly ever let me down. I've covered about twenty thousand miles by dog team in the last thirteen years, and I've walked home only once, when they took off without me.

That's a whole lot better than I could ask of any snow machine.

# 10

# DOG-TEAM HOLIDAY

**D**uring the warm, bright days of March, Miki and I pull off the trapline and go on vacation. Trail-hardened from the long winter's work and tired of going over the same trapping trails, we feel the need for a change.

For two or three weeks we travel, camping out at night and living out of a six-foot dogsled.

Certainly the most memorable trip we took was the one through Denali Park during spring break in our last year at the university, when we plummeted down snowdrifts and mountainsides, forded open streams and chased that grizzly. We had traveled about ninety miles in nine days. Later we found that, on a good trail, our team could go fifty miles a day without too much strain, but when we were breaking trail with snowshoes in front of the dogs, ten miles a day was a closer average.

Never was snowshoeing more tedious than on a trip we made to McGrath, a hundred and sixty miles from home. We started out with a heavy load, anticipating several days of trail-breaking, and after thirty miles on a snow machine trail we hit the unbroken trail leading to the village of Telida.

For five long days we snowshoed ahead of the dogs in very deep snow. For the first couple of days the sled was so heavily loaded with dog food that we had to snowshoe out and back and out again to pack the snow enough for the dogs to pull the sled forward. Daily wind and fresh snow did little to increase our appreciation of old-time North Country travel.

Finally, not far from the tiny Native village of Telida, we broke out onto wide, drifted Telida Lake. The dogs picked up the pace on the hard-packed drifts, and as we started across the lake we heard an airplane overhead.

Our parents, wondering why we had not yet phoned from Telida, had come out to check on us. As soon as they spotted us, they flew back home for a hundred and fifty pounds of dog and people food, which Daddy landed on the lake for us. We were down to oatmeal by then, and our gratitude was doubled because Daddy made the flight in the face of an oncoming snowstorm. The dogs, though they did not appreciate the renewed load, jumped on the big meal of dog food, tallow and liver they received that night.

Shortly after we picked up our supplies, we hit a broken snow-machine trail. It was one of the most exciting moments of my mushing career. After toiling ten hours a day for five days, going hardly a mile an hour, traveling effortlessly at seven miles an hour seemed incredible.

We reached the river called Swift Fork and turned right. Several miles later we realized we were going upstream. According to the map we needed to go downstream to reach Telida, but the scale was too small for us to tell which fork of the river we should go on. Not wanting to believe we were on the wrong trail, we went determinedly on. Maybe the sweepers in this river had all frozen drifting upstream!

"I smell smoke!" Miki said eagerly. "We must be getting close." But after several minutes of increasing darkness, we still saw no sign of the village.

"I do smell smoke," Miki insisted. "But maybe — oh, I think it's you!" From her position on skis behind the sled, fumes drifting back from my coat, drenched with campfire smoke, made her think of wood smoke from Telida.

By nightfall we knew we were on the wrong track. We camped, and the next day retraced our tracks and finally arrived at Telida. At that point we didn't know whether to continue our trip or just go home. Daddy had given us news that the year's biggest storm was forecast to bring a load of snow inland soon, and he'd also heard that the trail into the next village, Nikolai, wasn't open very often.

For the time being we were happy just to be in a dry, heated house. Our welcome in Telida was quiet but warm. The school's janitor, Dick Nikolai, and his wife, Oline, installed us in the school, which was vacant as the children had gone on a field trip to Fairbanks. We took the opportunity to dry our clothing and repair trail-worn gear. Then somebody told us a couple of men planned to come up from Nikolai by snow machine that very day and, elated, we decided to go on despite the forecasted blizzard.

In the evening one of the snow-machiners stepped into the schoolhouse. Steve Eluska was a slim Native with a thick shock of black hair and a voice that held laughter. He told us that he and his companion, Winchell Tichnor, had just broken out the fifty-mile trail to Nikolai, which apparently was not used regularly. We mentioned that we had cached some dog food at Telida Lake and needed to pick it up before going on in the morning. Later that night we found the feed stacked neatly outside the schoolhouse. The following day we set off for Nikolai, two hours ahead of schedule because of the time Steve had saved us.

In two days we reached Nikolai, where we knew a young woman named Agnes Tony through a mutual friend. Although she looked busy she invited us to stay with her and we accepted gratefully. Since last night had been windy and twenty below, I for one was glad to stay. Miki always slept comfortably in the sled under the sled tarp, but I slept beside the sled on a soft pile of spruce boughs, and an open wind generally cut through my sleeping bag if we weren't camped in a protected spot.

We asked around Nikolai for beaver carcasses we might buy to feed our dogs, and someone directed us to Sonny Holmberg. We decided before knocking at his door that we couldn't afford to pay more than fifteen dollars a carcass, even though the going price was usually twenty dollars or more. With the major sled races over by now, we hoped demand and prices would be down.

Sonny invited us into a small, neat kitchen and we got straight to business. The dark-featured trapper seemed surprised that we had ventured so far with our dogs. "Not many girls go out like that," he said. "They all stay home."

He was trapping beaver out of a line cabin fifteen miles from McGrath. "How many do you want?" he asked.

"Two or three, depending upon the price."

"I'd give you that many."

"We'd like to pay you for them," I said.

"No, I'll give them to you. I'll be up there tomorrow, but if you get there before I do, just tell my partner and he'll give them to you."

I couldn't believe we would get beaver meat for free! Riddled with fat and highly palatable, it is the best feed you can give a working dog. Miki asked Sonny whether he would sell us a few beaver pelts. We planned to spend March on the trail instead of trapping beaver, and we always needed a few skins for our small handcraft business. Sonny agreed to sell us some pelts on our way home. He kept looking at my gloves, which had been worn and tattered even before I'd burned the right one half up over the campfire a couple days earlier.

Finally he said, "Do you want another pair of gloves? I've got quite a few."

"Oh, I'm all right. I have my overmitts in the dogsled."

"But I've got a pair right here you can have."

"No, I'm fine." I looked at my hands, embarrassed. The gloves really were in pretty bad shape. There wasn't much left of the right one. "I'm fine," I said again, but Sonny still looked worried.

As we walked back to Agnes's house Miki said, "We ought to offer him a real good price for his beaver pelts, to make up for the carcasses he gave us."

We set off the next morning in ominous weather. Agnes led the way through town on her snow machine, guiding us to the Kuskokwim River and the famed Iditarod Trail which runs from Anchorage to Nome. The snowstorm moved in rapidly and we decided to make a dash for McGrath, nearly fifty miles away.

The Iditarod dogsled race had just passed by, and as we skimmed down the hard-packed trail we picked up the booties which had been thrown from the feet of some of the several hundred dogs in the race. At first we couldn't grab them as we went past because they had frozen to the snowy trail, and we'd each make an unsuccessful grab at every passing bootie. Then I started kicking them instead of grabbing them. Miki, skiing behind me, could then pick up the booties I knocked loose.

We picked up other things dropped by the racers,

including several bungee cords and a very nice digital time-piece. Then I saw a glove lying on the trail ahead.

"Please, please be a righty," I begged as we neared it. I grabbed and unfolded it. "It is! A brand-new righty!" I pulled off my tattered glove, and pulled on the new yellow work glove.

The snow began to fall seriously by the time we reached Sonny's cabin at three that afternoon. He asked us in for tea, but considering the heavy snow we thought it wise to push for McGrath. I picked up one beaver and we hurried on, planning to pick up two more on the way home.

The Iditarod Trail swings up onto a road near McGrath. According to the map we should turn left. According to the sled tracks coming up the trail, we should turn right.

"Our map's twenty years old, you know," Miki said. "This road is probably a newer road, not marked on the map."

"OK, we'll turn right, but it'll be your fault if we get lost and disappear from the face of the earth." A few minutes later we saw a big flock of ravens flying toward us over the road.

"This has to be the right way!" I cried jubilantly. "Here come the ravens, going home after a day's scrounging in the city!" It turned out the ravens were actually returning from the city dump, but after passing the dump we entered town and ran smack into one of the very few people we knew there. Diane Ketelson, a public health nurse, had invited us to stay with her, and now she directed us to her home. In a few minutes we had the dogs staked out in her yard. Inside her cozy little cabin we found a cluster of people whom Diane introduced as Lucky Egrass, a pilot and wolf hunter; Rudy Demoski, an Iditarod veteran; Ginger Cox, whom we already knew, and Ginger's friend Doug Bangs, an athlete and competitive skier. Late that evening I realized that, except for Lucky, they all were staying with Diane, whose home, though modern in every way, was small  for such a crowd.

We were concerned about overcrowding the household, especially when Ginger and Doug unrolled sleeping bags on the living-room floor while we took an upstairs bedroom, but Diane insisted it was no problem. Their congeniality did not cool even when we had to extend our visit to three days while waiting for the storm to blow over. Fog and low clouds hung over the small town and fourteen inches of fresh snow soon packed into slush as rain and drizzle moved in to batter the new accumulation.

We spread ourselves out by eating with the Magnusen family across the street, and with the Collins family downtown. The Magnusens are related to our dear friend Hazel Menke at home, and though the Collins family of McGrath bears no relation to us, we frequently receive each other's mail by mistake and so, though we had never met, it seemed we knew them well.

On the last day one of our huskies came in season and our dogs barked furiously the night through to keep strays at bay. We knew it was time to go.

When we left McGrath we had six inches of crusty cover to break through with skis in front of the toiling dogs. Ginger's friend Doug skied fifteen miles down to Sonny Holmberg's place to help us break trail, a thirty-mile round trip for him.

Sonny invited us in to lunch and after tomato soup, pilot bread and deliciously cooked beaver meat, we talked fur. He had several fine pelts, well scraped and large. After examining them I said, "Well, we've got two hundred dollars with us, so if we give you fifty bucks each, we can take four pelts."

At that time fifty dollars was a monsterous price and I knew it, but he'd given us all that beaver meat for free. Some years you can get a good price for beaver pelts, but that year the market hit rock bottom.

"Oh, I couldn't take that much," Sonny replied.

"I'd like to pay you back for the meat," I confessed.

"But if you pay me that much you won't be able to buy all of them," Sonny said. "Twenty-five dollars is fine."

"Twenty-five dollars! How about thirty-five?"

"I'd give them to you if I didn't need the money," Sonny insisted. "And that's all I'd get from the fur-buyer."

"How about thirty?"

"Twenty-five is fine," Sonny parried.

"We're not supposed to be bargaining like this," I protested.

Sonny laughed a little uneasily. "I'd give them to you if I didn't need the money," he repeated.

I paid him for six pelts at twenty-five dollars each. "I really appreciate it," I told him. What else could I say? I never was one to drive a hard bargain.

Doug asked for a loan so he could buy a beaver pelt too. I readily gave him the money though we hardly knew him, and the debt was repaid shortly. A couple years later we learned with regret that he had been drowned.

A warm front followed the storm and for two days Miki and I slogged through wet snow which soaked our feet during the first hour of every day. The first evening out, a ski plane landed on the river beside us and the pilot told us where we could find a cabin to stay the night. He said he had met us when we were little, when Daddy worked for the FAA, but he didn't tell us his name. After meeting him that time, I ran into him every single time I went to McGrath and he always came over to talk. I enjoyed him immensely and he did tell me his name at least once, but I could never remember it.

We did not reach the cabin that night, but camping out in the warm spring air was no hardship. Our flying friend gave me a warm feeling, not for the information he offered, but because he cared enough to drop down and give it to us.

During the night a snow machine passed. We followed

its broken trail on into Nikolai, spent the night outside of town, and passed through in the morning. At the store we learned that Steve Eluska had broken trail down from Telida with his snow machine so we could find our way over the vast marshes to his village.

I was incredulous. He made a hundred-mile round trip just to help us out? Although he later accepted the gas money we offered, he never asked for compensation. Miki and I headed out on his fresh trail, but the warm air softened it so badly we kept dropping through the three-foot snowpack, sinking clear to the ground. By midafternoon trail conditions were intolerable, so when we saw the sky clearing we camped. The clear sky meant a cold night, a freezing trail, and good going by morning.

Steve caught up with us on his snow machine as we settled in. He'd had trouble with the trail, too, especially where our sled had fallen through.

"I finally caught up with you guys," he said. "I kept thinking, oh, no, aren't they ever going to stop!"

Miki and I laughed uneasily. We felt bad that we'd messed up his nice trail.

"How deep was the overflow in the creek back there when you crossed it?" Steve asked.

"A few inches. How deep is it now?"

He made a grimace and indicated to his knee. The water had risen a foot in two hours. Steve's snow machine had bogged down in the water and he'd had a tussle pulling it out. The rising water was a sure sign of spring.

Steve spent the night in his sled near our camp and led the way into Telida early the next morning. The schoolteacher, Helen Frost, a sweet, dark-haired young woman, asked us to supper and let us spend another warm night in her schoolhouse.

We still had sixty miles to go. We expected to break trail all the way back to Minchumina, but just a few miles outside Telida, Daddy roared up on his Ski-Doo. He had broken out forty-five miles of trail for us. He brought a beaver carcass for the dogs, a gift from Tom Flood, a trapper and long-time friend. Arriving home the next day, we stopped by the Post Office to thank his wife Mary, the Minchumina postmaster.

Although trail conditions at times proved difficult, they lacked the drama of some trips and had it not been for the people along the way, I would have little to remember. It seemed everyone in Alaska was out to speed us along our way that year.

The following year we spent less time on the trail but traveled twice as far, thanks to excellent trail conditions. This time Steve Eluska, ever the obliging friend, broke trail for us all the way to Minchumina for the cost of the gas, so instead of taking a week to reach Telida, we did the sixty miles in one day. From there we went to McGrath and on out the Iditarod Trail.

We planned to visit Jim and Kath Flemings and their family, who lived twenty-five miles up a river off the Iditarod Trail. There we ran into tough conditions. Our old leader, Loki, was incapacitated after one of his numerous dogfights, so young Ivanhoe had his first real test as a leader. The sensitive dog looked surprised when we asked him to lead the team off the Iditarod Trail onto the trackless river. He didn't know what to do, so he followed animal tracks up the river instead of cutting his own trail into the blank snow. He didn't have the sense to follow the wolf tracks, which took the easiest and straightest route. Oh, no. He followed otter tracks, which slid under sweepers along the bank, poked into holes and ducked under logs. Loki was disgusted.

Then we ran into water. With an early spring upon us, the creek had begun to flood. An inch of ice had formed over the water and for awhile we went all right, but the overflow grew deeper and then the sled started breaking through to the main creek ice below.

"Hike, Ivanhoe!" I roared. "Hike! Dad-gum it!" The dog kept balking at the water's edge. We ran through water off and on for several miles and sometimes Ivanhoe would go through it. Sometimes he wouldn't.

"There goes Loki," Miki said. As usual, she was skijoring on a rope behind the sled while I drove the team. Loki cut wide around my five dogs, growling as he darted past Ivanhoe, and led the way along the edge of the overflow, expertly staying on the best ice and positively radiating an aura of disdain for the younger dog. Ivanhoe turned and followed him.

When we ran into bank-to-bank water, though, Loki abandoned Ivanhoe to his own resources and bounded up the bank to travel in the dense trees, where no sled could follow. Ivanhoe tried to follow him, but we forced him to struggle on up the creek. We made good time where the overflow was frozen, but got colder and wetter each time we ran into water, which came in deeper and longer stretches. Ivanhoe started getting discouraged. He plainly thought this was pointless, and we were on the verge of agreeing. Miki's feet, in ankle-high ski boots, were soaked and getting cold.

"Waterskiing," I laughed, but after awhile it wasn't so funny. My feet were soaked, too, but my heavier Bean boots kept them warmer. Thankfully our traditional-style basket sled kept our load above the water. The toboggan sleds in common use these days are good for plenty of things, but not for going through water.

Miki's feet grew colder as the water poured past her boots without letup. The pressure of the current against her ankles sometimes forced water up to her knees. I could jump up onto the sled to avoid most of it. The colder her feet got, the more bitterly she complained. I felt bad, but couldn't help observing: "They can't freeze, you know! It's forty-five above!"

"They *hurt*, all right?" Miki shouted. But she skied on,

as always. Every bend brought more and more water, until we were in it more than out of it.

"Ivanhoe!" I roared hoarsely every time the poor dog tried to climb into the bushes out of the water. "Gee! Gee! Ivanhoe!"

We paused at last, breathless from the cold. Ivanhoe glared reproachfully over his shoulder. Breakup was in full swing, and we had to think about getting back down this river, too. But had we come three hundred miles only to be turned back practically at Jim's doorstep?

"Stop!" Miki cried. "Shh!" We held our breaths, hearts pounding. Even the dogs stopped panting to listen. Then, through the burbling sounds of spring, we heard dogs barking. Jim's dogs. A moment later we heard voices back in the trees and Jim's sons, Shawn and Jimmy, appeared in the brush.

"Is there a trail back there?" I shouted, rather more vehemently than necessary.

"Yes," they called. We were there!

Twenty minutes later we sat warm and cozy in Jim's house with his family, laughing at our troubles as the memory already turned from bitter to sweet. Miki impressed them all by recounting the names of Jim's dogs from memory — this at the request of our special friend, Bumper, Jim's daughter. We'd been introduced to the big huskies only once before, and I certainly didn't remember their names.

We had planned to stay a day with the Flemings to rest the dogs, but with breakup coming so fast we decided to leave early the next morning. Jim had an overland trail which led us around the worst of the water, and we camped that afternoon at the base of the Beaver Mountains. Again we hoped to rest the dogs for a day, but with bare tundra exposed on the mountain flanks, one more day could make the going intolerable. We rose at three and traveled during the colder early-morning hours.

Halfway through the Beaver Mountains, just as the dawn began to turn from gray to pink, I caught an airborne scent. With a lurch of the heart I said to Miki, "I smell smoke!"

We stared at each other and then both said, "Oh, no!"

A shelter cabin lay a mile ahead, and we guessed that two lagging Iditarod racers were holed up there. We had no desire to visit them, but we couldn't slip past because we had some dog feed cached there.

We pulled up outside the plywood shack at six in the morning. The two men were there, all right, the only racers left on that stretch of trail. Though already disqualified, they continued the trek to Nome with admirable though questionable determination. They were notorious for their lack of professionalism.

One man rose to greet us. The other, who'd been badly frostbitten early in the race, stayed in bed. Why they remained there during the cool morning hours was beyond me. By noon everything would be melting, trails mushy, dogs overheating.

We picked up our cached feed and rushed away quickly, passed through the mountains before the heat of the day, and camped at one p.m. not far from the ghost town of Ophir. Early the next morning we sped on into the sparsely populated mining camp and there met Robbie Roberts, a veteran musher. We found him loading up to pull out ahead of the annual Innoko River flood.

"You want some dog food?" we asked. "We've got a bunch left over because the trails were so fast, and we don't want to haul it all the way to McGrath."

"No, I got too much stuff to haul out already," Robbie told us. "I got a bunch of leftover Iditarod dog food, if you want any. How come you use that polypro for your towline? You know how easy it breaks at forty below? You got a lame dog?" He looked at Loki.

"Yeah, he cut his foot in a fight."

"Ever tried VetWrap?" He gave us two rolls. "You cut real thin strips and use Superglue to seal it over a cut and hold it shut." Robbie talked nonstop. "You meet those two Iditaroders out there?"

"Yeah, we saw them at Don's cabin."

Robbie laughed. "They spent the other night here and told me to get them up early, so I did, but they messed around until eleven o'clock. You know when they got to McGrath, they tied their teams stretched straight across the main street in front of the A.C. [Alaska Commercial Company] store. Couldn't anybody get past them."

Robbie went on and on. We liked him immensely.

But the morning grew warm, so we took our reluctant leave and pushed the dogs and our heavy load over the mountains to Takotna. There at last we found someone to take our extra dog food, a musher who had some dogs we were interested in. As we started to unload the sled, he stopped us.

"Let's see how much weight you really have there," he said a little skeptically. He started to pick up the back end of the sled by the handlebow, but couldn't even get it off the ground.

I laughed. "Now you see why we want to dump it!"

"You sure you want to give it away? All this expensive Iams Eukanuba?" he asked doubtfully.

"Please, *please* don't make us pull it over Takotna Mountain!" I begged.

We dumped the stuff before he could stop us, and hurried away to reach McGrath by nightfall. Without the extra load we traveled fast despite our small team, and in just a few days we were home again. We had stopped briefly in Telida to thank Helen Frost again, and buy some beaver carcasses from Steve Eluska and his father. The veteran old trapper liked us, but said we were too thin for him. (Ha ha!)

Frequently at the start of a trip our dogs get irritable, the weather is lousy, and the sled is self-destructing, but after a few days' travel all is going well again.

"Bad start, good finish," they say.

That axiom proved true for us again on a recent trip to Fairbanks. Feeling financially mortified, we decided to mush rather than fly. It's a 380-mile round trip, relatively short compared to some of our trips, which sometimes stretch more than a thousand miles.

We had ten dogs running loose in harness, and we called them to the sled one at a time to hook them to the towline. With nine dogs hooked up, I had to walk back to the dogs' yard to find our leader, Legs. He abhorred the chaos of hooking up, and generally hid in his house until it was over. Miki was standing on the snow hook to keep the eager dogs anchored.

I was on my way back with Legs when I saw the dogs bolt down the steep hill to the lake, dragging Miki. Our spare snow hook, a poor design and in use only because we'd recently lost the good one, had popped out while Miki was standing on it. She had belly-flopped onto a little sled tied behind the dogsled, and was careening down the hill behind the galloping dogs.

At a vertical snowbank at the bottom of the hill, the uncontrolled dogsled flew into the air, snapped sideways and rolled. Dog food, gear and groceries flew far and wide. The hand sled snapped up behind the dogsled, and Miki parted company with it in midair. She staggered to her feet and went to the dogs, who had stopped when the sled rolled. Slowly she set the hook and picked up the sled.

Many times I had seen my sister take a spill, roll on the ground, then walk hunched over like that, only to pull herself together and go on. This time was different. As I approached the sled I saw blood spattered on the ground.

"Is that *your* blood?" I demanded to know.

"Yeah, I guess so. It's just a bloody nose." She paused, considering. "I seem to have bashed a tooth in. No, two teeth. Maybe three or four."

I stared at her. Miki has strong, healthy teeth. So do I, but mine frequently got broken — like the time a horse kicked me in the mouth, and the time I punched myself in the face with an iron snow hook. Things like that just didn't happen to Miki.

She stood running her tongue over her teeth and then added, "And my upper gums feel like pudding." She paused, then asked anxiously, "Do you think we should fly to town? It doesn't hurt . . . I want to go on with the dogs, but . . . I mean, this could affect me for the rest of my life."

She wanted me to tell her to fly to town right now and  see a dentist, but with the dogs hooked up and the sled loaded, I really wanted to go on. I couldn't say the words. She had to make the decision.

"I guess I'd better fly to town," she said mournfully.

"I'll take you in," I offered.

We unhooked the dogs, went into the house, and made an abashed confession to our parents. Marmee got onto the ham radio and made a dental appointment for Miki. Daddy and I dug the Cessna out of the snow, heated the engine, put in some gas and taxied to a smooth area on the lake. Miki and I flew to Fairbanks.

Next day I returned home alone to run the dogs to town by myself while Miki convalesced. I spent a day and a half breaking twenty miles of trail, snowshoeing in front of the dogs in deep, wet snow. Then we hit hard-packed trail. The dogs gave a collective gasp, started to run, and didn't slow down much. We made the hundred and ten miles to Nenana in sixteen hours, including rest breaks every fifteen minutes to keep the dogs from overheating in the forty-degree weather.

Miki met me with the folks' truck in Nenana. The

dentist had patched her teeth with stitches and wire, and he'd kept calling her Julie, he was so used to working on me. She was in pretty good shape after a six-day rest. We trucked the dogs to Fairbanks, ran a five-month accumulation of errands, then mushed home again. Miki skijored behind the dogsled all the way home, going up and down hills and banks, through flooding creeks, across glare ice and bare tundra with her usual dexterity.

Bad start, good finish.

The axiom changed to "bad start, bad finish" when we decided to give racing a try.

# 11

# BAD START, BAD FINISH

Let's face it folks: You can't win dogsled races with seventy-pound trapline dogs, any more than you could win the Kentucky Derby with a Belgian draft horse. Our dogs are ideal for trapline work, but they are trapline dogs. Why try them out on the longest cross-country dog race in the world?

I always held Tok responsible for sparking my interest in the Iditarod. His former owner had run him in the race, and when Julie and I were seniors in high school we ran him and Loki around town, mostly skijoring with one dog apiece. Good as Tok was, Loki was better. He was faster, a more aggressive worker, and had more stamina. So if Tok could run the Last Great Race, Loki could run it better. All we had to do was come up with eight or ten more just like him.

That dream was to hold me for years. I was very serious

about it, but I was realistic, too. I didn't set any goals. I just figured when we had the right team, I'd run the race. I knew I wouldn't have a competitive team, but for two-thirds of the Iditarod racers the goal is to reach Nome, more than a thousand miles from the start in Anchorage. They don't hope to win.

After seeing how well those few dogs did on the long trip west of McGrath in 1983, I figured 1984 would be the year. We had raised a couple of nice pups, bought two dogs, and had two more dumped on us by another Iditarod musher who was cleaning out his dog yard. We ran eleven dogs on the trapline that year. Some didn't perform so well as I'd have liked, but they were all we had. Finding good dogs of that size seemed nearly impossible.

In January Harold's Air Service flew us, dogs, sled and all to Fairbanks, where we planned to train until race time. The slow trails of the trapline make slow dogs, and we needed to work on their speed more than anything else. In Fairbanks we found an abundance of well-packed, fast snow-machine trails.

We also found an abundance of cold weather. Most of January the temperatures hovered between twenty and forty below, and although we ran the dogs anyway, the cold took the fun out of it for both us and the dogs.

A new rule on the Iditarod required rookie mushers to finish a two-hundred-mile race to qualify. I heard that Mitch Demientieff, a rookie musher in Nenana, was putting together a qualifying race consisting of two round trips between Nenana and Minto, four fifty-two-mile legs. I called Mitch on the phone and signed up. This would not be a very stressful race, and I merely wanted to finish. We were scheduled to run in mid-January, but the race was postponed for a week due to severe weather. That meant it had to be run just four weeks before the start of the Iditarod. The dogs wouldn't have much time to recover.

Chapter Eleven ● Bad Start, Bad Finish

The temperature climbed to twenty below. Mitch called me at our folks' house in Fairbanks.

"If you can get down here by five p.m. we'll go," he said.

"I'll be there!" I had two hours. After loading the dogs into the truck and driving the sixty miles to Nenana, I had just time to ready the sled and hitch up the dogs. The Race Marshall began counting down even as I snapped the last dog into place, and by the time I was back on the runners he shouted, "*Go!*"

Darkness came only an hour later. Mitch ran just ahead of me and Russ and Wayne, the other two racers, followed somewhere behind. As I adjusted my headlamp to the oncoming blackness, the wind began picking up.

Young Ivanhoe ran in the lead. Loki, my only other trained leader at the time, had a sprained shoulder and I'd left him at home. Ivanhoe was sharp, fast and a good gee-haw dog, but he lacked trail savvy and he didn't push himself. I was surprised that my big trapline dogs kept up with Mitch's team. They weren't used to traveling with other teams and they weren't about to fall back.

Julie and I had mushed nearly to Old Minto, halfway to New Minto, on a training run. From there I followed the sparkle of Mitch's headlamp into the dark unknown. I stopped only once, to give each dog a small chunk of meat.

By midnight the wind worsened and snow began falling in thick flurries. The gusts hit thirty or forty miles an hour as we pushed northward into the face of the blizzard. The temperature had not warmed with the storm, and at twenty-five below the wind chill dropped to about eighty-five below. After frostbite the previous winter my cheeks remained sensitive to the cold, and now my chin threatened to freeze as well. Every few minutes I had to slip my hand from the warm beaver overmitts to take the chill off my face. But my heavy parka, fur mukluks and big overalls kept the rest of me snug and warm.

Mitch let me take the lead. His dogs, tiring from pushing through the thickening snow, needed a break. But Ivanhoe just didn't know what he was doing. He lost the trail as soon as we headed out across a drifted lake. We wasted time searching for it. Mitch finally located the track and took the lead again. I think one of his leaders had been on the Minto trail before and knew the way. By then Russ caught up and followed just behind me.

The wind howled across Minto Flats, pushing snow before it, whipping across the lakes and drifting in the trail. My light picked up flashing flakes of snow, the silvery backs of my dogs and, if I looked straight down, an occasional runner scratch in the wind-packed surface. Beyond that I couldn't see much at all.

The wind sucked away the dogs' spirit and drained their strength. When I stopped to straighten a tangled line some miles on, Mitch pulled away and I didn't catch up again. Ivanhoe had to pick up the trail now instead of just following the team ahead. Russ and I passed each other several times, and then he too went on when I stopped with another tangle.

Because of the screaming wind I could work barehanded only for moments at a time. The battery of my headlamp was dying in the cold and I couldn't see the lines very well. When I finally started on, Ivanhoe kept leaving the trail. I had to stop, lead him back, untangle the traces and start on again, only to have him cut off to the left once more. I did not realize then that he was trying to follow a parallel trail a few yards away, probably one with Mitch's scent still fresh on it.

I didn't know where I was nor how far I had to go. Except for a few willows I saw no sign of any break from the wind. If I followed the wrong trail in the dark, or if Ivanhoe took me off bush-bucking, I could be in real trouble. I knew if I got lost I'd never find the right trail until daylight, assuming I even knew I was lost. With a fading headlamp I couldn't pick out the faint tracks of Mitch's sled. I had either to push on and hope Ivanhoe followed the right trail, or camp in the howling wind until daylight brought the answers.

The light of a snow machine far ahead brought instant relief. The people of Minto, growing concerned, sent out snow machiners to find the dog teams. We'd left Nenana more than eight hours ago and Mitch had expected to reach Minto in only five or six hours.

Ivanhoe was reluctant at first to follow the snow machine back toward Minto. He still smelled Mitch's tracks on the parallel trail and knew we were supposed to follow them, but finally I convinced him of what I needed. Usually pacing a dog team with a motorized vehicle is against the rules, but under the circumstances I don't think anyone complained about it.

With no trees to break the wind, it came hurtling down the river, slamming into the team with frightening velocity. The snowflakes whipped around thick and fast as the dogs fought to maintain their footing in the gale. The gusts hit fifty miles an hour, carrying windblown snow high in the air and the temperature, if anything, fell lower.

A little shock rushed through me when I brushed a bare hand across my cheek and felt the skin crinkle in a frozen sheet beneath my fingers. I huddled down on the runners behind the sled, pulling my parka hood and fur ruff close around my face. Every few minutes I looked up to make sure Ivanhoe stayed on course, and in the short seconds I held my face up to the wind the thin sheet of ice reformed on my cheeks and chin. I didn't realize until the next day that it was just snow freezing onto my face, not the flesh itself freezing.

In places the wind had scoured the river ice bare, leaving a slick surface. As the dogs slipped across the glassy ice the gusts knocked them clear off their feet, and when my sled hit the ice the wind slammed it sidewise, snapping around my hundred-and-twenty-pound wheel dogs, Comet and Streak. Sometimes half the team was whipped around before the sled hit snow again. I stayed down behind the sled, trying to keep the blizzard off my face and lessen the resistance my body created. But despite the weariness and the rather frightful situation, deep inside of me glowed a small, warm spark of triumph: even with a wind chill factor of a hundred degrees below zero, only my exposed face felt cold.

Minto. The lights shone welcomingly down from the bluffs, piercing the blinding wind and snow. I arrived just after three a.m., fifteen minutes behind Mitch. Russ, who had passed me an hour earlier, was not there. Searchers finally found him ten miles back, lost in the whiteout. Of Wayne, the fourth and last musher, there was no sign.

I put the dogs in a slight gully, partially protected from the wind, fed them, watered them, and did what I could to make them comfortable. I caught a few hours' rest on a sofa in the lodge. By nine in the morning Mitch was ready to go and I followed him back out into the wind.

In some ways the return trip was harder. Traveling downwind, the cold seemed much less severe, and in the daylight Mitch's dogs picked up the trail with little trouble. But twelve inches of snow had fallen during the night and pushing through the deep powder wore the dogs down. Ivanhoe pushed on until he fell off the hard-packed surface of the trail under the new snow, and then made no attempt to find the trail again. I tried every dog that might go, leader or not, but in the end Mitch broke trail nearly the whole way. I felt badly about it; if I'd had Loki. . .

Nightfall found us only halfway back to Nenana and Mitch walking ahead of his dogs to find the trail for them. We camped when darkness and drifts hid the last traces of the buried trail. Russ caught up with us, and Wayne, who'd run into us after having spent the first night out, joined us for the return trip to Nenana, where he would scratch from the race.

By the following morning people were concerned about Wayne, unsighted so far as they knew since he'd left Nenana two days ealier. A Search and Rescue team was called out, and by eleven half a dozen snow machines, two dogs teams and a helicopter converged on us, guaranteeing us a broken trail.

I passed Mitch fifteen miles out of Nenana. His dogs had fared badly breaking trail the day before, and I felt ashamed to take advantage of the situation, but I couldn't keep holding my dogs back. When I pulled into Nenana a small group of people gathered to watch the teams come in. I won the first round, but I don't think anyone was more surprised than I. My dogs just aren't cut out for racing. The second round held more surprises, only this time the joke was on me.

I left Nenana for the second trip to Minto twelve hours later, six hours behind Russ and Mitch. I was worried about the dogs. I dropped one with a limp, and I knew the others weren't going to be very happy about heading out that trail again. Mitch had expressed surprise that I wasn't going to try to hold my lead.

"Mitch," I said, "The Iditarod starts in less than four weeks. If it started tomorrow I'd leave Anchorage with nine dogs, and one would be in the basket."

He looked a little taken back. I don't think he realized just how serious my dog situation was. I didn't either.

The dogs moved sluggishly as I headed out an hour before dawn on the third day. I had to jump on a couple to get them going, but we made it into Old Minto in two hours' less time than the fellows ahead of me. I stopped for an hour, watered and fed my dogs, changed their booties, spent a couple moments with each one, and choked down part of a sandwich.

The dogs wouldn't go on. They just refused to get up.

I let them rest another hour and tried again. They balked. I stood each one up, but by the time I was two pairs up from the sled, my wheelers were off the trail lying the snow again. Flip, bothered by a bone spur in his back, as I discovered later, refused even to stand up. Ivanhoe tightened up on command, but wouldn't even try to drag the rest of the team to get them started. He just didn't have the powerful character required of a truly fine leader.

For six hours I alternately rested the dogs and tried to get them up. If I'd been alone I might have flogged every one of them, but with people staying in the cabin, I couldn't. Not only would that have looked bad, it could have disqualified me. I knew the dogs were taking advantage of me, but they had never done anything like this before and I just didn't know how to handle it. In the end they won. We spent the night right there. Mitch arrived that evening on his way back to Nenana, his face etched with fatigue, and he stayed too. He went on the following day to win the race.

The dogs were still balky in the morning. Comet, always prone to wrist sprains, had a foreleg swell up and go bad during the night and he could hardly hobble along. For two or three hours I walked alongside of or ahead of the dogs, sometimes dropping back to walk behind the sled. They finally loosened up in mind and body and I could pedal with one foot on the runners.

Russ scratched at Minto when his dogs got sick, so I was in second place and the last musher left in the race. I spent the night in the lodge, slept a luxurious eight hours, ate a good breakfast with Lefty Jimmie, left Comet with Luke Titus, and headed back for Nenana.

The dogs knew they were going home. Although I had to baby them along occasionally, and they even threatened to camp at Old Minto again, I could pedal instead of walk and they were willing to keep moving. I sang song after song until my voice gave out, trying to buoy their spirits and ease the tension between us. The wind had picked up again and I broke open the heavily drifted trail for forty-five miles. Maybe I was just tired, but it seemed I'd never felt the sled drag so hard as it did on some of those cold, hard-packed drifts. Finally, long after dark, we reached sheltering trees again, ten miles from Nenana.

Even after ten hours of pushing through those drifts, when the dogs hit that good trail they doubled their pace and clipped along through the darkness. They lacked the unity and power they'd once had, but they knew they were going home and nothing could stop them. Outside the cone of silvery light from my headlamp it was very dark and very cold. The frost started to creep into my cheek again. I pulled a hand out of my overmitts and, still pedaling, pressed it against my face, feeling the small, hard lump melt and vanish. The metal frame of my glasses stuck to the skin, but I couldn't tell whether it was frozen there or glued on by the dried blood oozing from the irritated frostbite.

"Home, James!" I cried out hoarsely. The dogs broke into a lope for a short distance, then slowed again to a mile-eating trot. Several times I stopped to let them breathe, and each time Streak toppled over on his side, gasping and panting, but after seconds of rest he'd bound to his feet at my word and pull his best until the next break.

No one was around when I slid across the wide Tanana River and came up the bank into Nenana at nine o'clock on that night of the fifth day of the race. Elsewhere in Alaska, two-hundred-mile races were being completed with winning times of under twenty-four hours. I punched my own time card and tied up the dogs, taking off their icy harnesses but leaving them snapped onto the towline. Julie had driven the truck back to Fairbanks. I found a phone and called her collect. She knew I'd left Minto that morning, and she knew what was going on.

I had come in second, by default since two of the four mushers scratched. I felt happy with second place, upset that my dogs, for the first time in ten years of mushing, had quit on me. I was proud and grateful to Streak, disgusted with Ivanhoe, and worried about Flip and several other dogs. I was weary and run-down, five pounds lighter than I'd been five days earlier, elated at having qualified for the Iditarod despite the grueling conditions, and terrified for fear I had wrecked my team to do so. I heard Julie accepting the charges, and then she said, "Yo!"

"Yeah," I croaked. "Turn off the TV and get down here."

"Right," she laughed, and hung up.

I laughed too. The first race was over.

I had three and a half weeks before the start of the Iditarod. Julie and I rushed through the food shipments for the race checkpoints, giving the dogs several days off. The next time we ran them I was not happy with their performance. Several of the dogs had problems and we brought some to the vet. Sparky, an outstanding year-old pup, had diabetes insipidus, which meant her kidneys weren't functioning properly. X-rays showed a bone spur in Flip's back. Another dog, whom we'd been treating for hypothyroidism, wasn't responding well to her medication. Julie retrieved Comet from Minto, and his sprain lingered for days.

Most mushers running the Iditarod pick the best fourteen to eighteen dogs out of a dog yard of fifty to a hundred or more. I had to pick eleven out of eleven.

I don't think I've been so depressed since I'd been coping with high school in town. I remember sitting on the floor of the basement, driving screws into the basket of my beautiful new sled, and the tears started running down my face. I didn't see how those dogs would ever get to Nome under race conditions. If I had not already sent out the food shipment, I might have withdrawn, but it was too late. I stood to lose not only the hundreds of dollars spent on the food shipment, but the months of training, time lost from trapping, and money invested in the dogs, not to mention the entry fee of more than a thousand dollars. I also had commitments to my sponsors — Katmai Harness Shop had provided me with booties, harnesses and other tack; Harold's Air had delivered us safely to Fairbanks free of charge, and several smaller sponsors had donated their time and money.

Julie knew I was depressed but we didn't talk about it much. To most people the name of the 1,049-mile sled-dog race from Anchorage to Nome might conjur up images of hard-working huskies, heroic mushers, blinding snowstorms or the awesome beauty of Rainy Pass. For me, after working for it for seven years, the Iditarod turned from a dream to a bad dream to a nightmare.

On the drive to Anchorage, with two sleds, eleven dogs and all my gear, the rear wheel tore off the truck. The first night in Anchorage two dogs broke loose and got into the first fight we'd had all year. Rusty, one of my best team dogs, came up so lame afterward that he could not walk. He did not pass the vet check, but he improved rapidly and was cleared at the start of the race. I had one dog with hypothyroidism, one with a bone spur, one with diabetes insipidus. Loki was recovering from his sprained shoulder. Comet was no longer limping, but I figured his leg hadn't strengthened yet. The temperature was forty-five above and after the cold training season, my heavy-coated dogs were gasping in the heat. So many things went wrong we started laughing about it. We had to. If we hadn't laughed we would have cried, and we don't like to cry.

I left Anchorage at 10:52 on March 3, Number fifty-six out of more than sixty mushers, so discouraged I hardly cared what happened beyond the well-being of my dogs. For the first three days I mushed through drizzling rain, and the heat dragged my dogs down until I was at the very last. By the time I reached Finger Lake, Jackson was limping as a result of a dogfight and Comet's leg was bothering him.

I lay in my sleeping bag on the dogsled, listening to the mist from the sodden sky, and thought about the day's happenings. The forty-five miles from Skwentna had taken nine hours. Another musher and I had arrived long after dark, tired and wet. His team got into a dogfight; lines tangled and choked one dog to death. I was haunted by the image of the musher, bent over his faithful worker and companion.

I mushed through Rainy Pass in the darkness of the following night, scrambling over fresh avalanches across the trail. Even in the dark the splendor was not lost on me as the dogs trotted smoothly along at three a.m. The trail travels up a narrow, V-shaped valley with pinnacles towering darkly above on either side. The beams of headlamps pinpointed other mushers. Despite the stories I'd heard about the difficulty of the grade, my powerful trapline dogs made the climb to the three-thousand-foot level easily.

Daylight found us twisting back down Dalzell Canyon, zigzagging back and forth across the tiny creek, crashing down ten-foot banks and dodging open holes where the ice had collapsed into the water. This place too produced many horror stories, but with my easy-going team and maneuverable stanchion sled, I passed through safely — with the help of Lady Luck. Then, from behind, I heard a shout.

Looking back I saw Dave Aisenbrey's sled upside-down in a gaping hole in the ice. I stopped quickly, anchored my dogs, and sprinted back to help him heave the toboggan back onto the trail. The rushing water was only knee-deep, but still plenty cold enough for me to appreciate staying out of it. Midmorning found us at Rohn Roadhouse, once a stop for freight teams traveling to and from the Interior but now just a trapper's cabin.

Mushers are required to take at least one twenty-four-hour break at one of the twenty checkpoints along the race trail. I'd planned on spending mine with friends in McGrath, but I had so much dog trouble I stayed at Rohn. We'd made it over Rainy Pass into the Interior, but Comet, after pulling with all his overwhelming dedication, could go no farther. I'd known Comet and Streak would not make it all the way; in fact, I'd figured on dropping them both at McGrath. Still, the loss of his marvelous presence was a blow, more to my spirits than anything else. Jackson had wrenched his shoulder again during the descent from the pass, but I hoped a day of rest might keep him in the team.

Traveling with two other mushers, I departed for Farewell the following afternoon. The twenty miles took until seven the following morning. The South Fork of the Kuskokwim was flooding and I followed Bob Sunder, who dragged his dogs through knee-deep water. My dogs had run through so much water on our trapline, they just couldn't be bothered by this crossing. Then we faced eighteen miles of bare ground, flooded trail and overflowed lakes. We could not travel at night without risk of losing the trail in the bare, unmarked terrain. By the time we reached Farewell, Bob, Dave Aisenbrey and I were a full day behind the other trail mushers. (In spite of what seemed to me to be an unbearably slow pace, at every checkpoint we were told that, compared to previous years, we were the fastest "tail-enders" to go through.)

Fortunately snow conditions improved as we headed out across the forty-mile Burn, a stretch devastated by a forest fire several years earlier. For once luck favored us. The Burn, often snowless and rough, wore a thick layer of snow and a smooth trail over the rough, deadfall-covered ground. We rested the dogs in the heat of the afternoon, and in the early evening I took the lead as the cooler weather perked up my dogs. The three of us weren't racing any more, and I was more than willing to take over the chore of breaking trail when Bob's smaller dogs tired. I always think it's funny how many people complain about a little snow on the trail or a steep climb. I've seen a few awful trails, but not on the Iditarod! After all the stories I'd heard about breaking sleds and getting lost in the Burn, the crossing seemed quite painless, if tiring on top of the previous miserable day.

Holy Moses, it felt good to be back in Kusko country! We reached the little Native village of Nikolai on the Kusko-kwim River some time past midnight, but one of the first people I saw was Helen Frost, the teacher from Telida, and her welcoming face was a warming sight. I was sorry to miss the Telida kids, who had come over to watch the race, but they had thoughtfully left a pitcher of grape juice, which seemed doubly delicious coming from friends and after the burning, dehydrating sun during the day. After carrying Jackson for twenty miles I gave him up as a lost cause, dropped him there, and went on to McGrath very early the following morning with nine dogs.

The stretch of trail unraveled bend after bend, bringing fond memories of the trips Julie and I had made through there, and the friends and acquaintances who came to greet me as I pulled into McGrath delighted me.

The dogs seemed happy enough, but I knew they were in bad shape. Two or three were dragging as much as pulling but I wasn't sure I could afford to go on with only seven dogs. My biggest mistake during the race proved to be not dropping the bum dogs fast enough — I didn't realize I couldn't afford *not* to drop them.

After fifteen luxurious hours with Sally Collins, including a bath, three large pieces of wedding cake left from her son Joel's wedding that very day, and nine hours of sound sleep, I followed Bob Sunder back out across the Kuskokwim and up into the hills toward Takotna and Ophir.

We passed both checkpoints by nightfall, spending a short time in each place, taking advantage of the hospitality poured on us at our every stop. Even for us, dragging along after fifty or sixty other mushers had already passed through, the welcome was warm. The cafe in Takotna passed out free coconut cream pie and lemonade, quenching the burning thirst I'd developed during the hot morning. At Ophir we were fed soup and sandwiches. I met our friend Robbie Roberts there, and he can talk dogs faster and better than anyone else I've ever met.

Dunk the dogs in water when they get too hot, he advised. Don't let them lie in the sun after working or they'll stiffen up. Give them lots of small breaks and they'll run happier and faster. Did I build my sled? At my nod, he demanded, wasn't it awfully heavy? and frowned at me with sharp blue eyes as I blushed. Despite the criticism I devoured his words, and in those fifteen minutes I learned more from Robbie than I could from a year's experience on the trail. Yet the most important hint he gave seemed to go over my head until I thought about it days later.

"If he isn't pulling, get rid of him," he said. "Don't keep a dog on your team if he isn't doing his share."

I think it was already too late.

We moved on in the blackness, paralleling the Innoko River. Sparky, the young dog with diabetes insipidus, was in season and several of the males were fighting. Three dogs started dragging — Mitsy, with hypothyroidism, was developing a false pregnancy; Flip's bone spur pained him, and Ivanhoe too lagged. He later proved to have inflamed wrists. I moved Sky up front. Although an untrained leader, he kept the team moving, and with his speed and Loki's ability, they did all right.

But during the third dogfight of the evening, two dogs joined up against my good old leader and tore him up pretty good. I left him in harness until he was dragging so badly I had to load him into the sled.

"You should've left him in the team so he wouldn't stiffen up so much," said Dr. Jim Leach, the trail vet at Cripple.

I could have cried.

The remainder of that night and the following day into Cripple had been quite horrible. At times I was walking in front of the dogs, coaxing them along. Sparky, although pulling gamely, became dehydrated. Streak limped along on sore feet, but I put him up in swing, right behind little blue-eyed Sky. Sky started forward on command and Streak would drag the rest of the dogs until they began to move and pull the sled. Streak knew he was pulling balky dogs instead of an honest load and he resented it deeply, but he knew I needed him. I needed him badly and he was always there for me. Of all our dogs, he and Loki are the only ones from whose eyes shine that special spark of power and dedication, and he came through for me every time. If he hadn't, I might still be out there.

When I reached Cripple the vet took Streak's temperature and told me he had a fever of 104 degrees, caused by a systemic infection from his tattered feet.

Only three dogs, Sky, Rusty, and one-year-old Amber remained in good health.

If I went on, I couldn't take Loki nor the three dragging dogs. That left five, the minimum number allowed under race rules. I might make it to Ruby on the Yukon, another hundred miles, but if I did push on, Sparky, with her bad kidneys, might die of dehydration. And I knew neither she nor Streak could go on from there.

For a day and a half I stayed in Cripple hoping for an improvement, but none came except for Streak's declining temperature following a massive dose of antibiotics. When I sat down with him in the snow he gazed at me with his steady golden-brown eyes. He was Loki's son and I knew he would pull until he dropped. I saw in his eyes that same special spark his father had, the profound trust he had in me, the absolute faith that I was not going to ask him to do something he could not.

I reached down and hugged him tight, and then quietly went inside and, through the tears in my eyes, signed the check-in sheet and wrote "Scratched."

After flying the team home and trying to settle down again, Julie and I overhauled our dog yard. Streak and Comet, despite their limitations as racers, were just too wonderful to get rid of. Flip and Jackson we gave to Steve Eluska in Telida, and they passed from our lives without regret. Ivanhoe, we gave to a recreational musher and hoped his wrist problems would improve with the lighter work. Dear Mitsy went to a friend in Fairbanks to live as a pet. Loki, slowed by age, retired to the less demanding if more exasperating task of training pups.

We kept Sparky in the house. She drank literally gallons every day, but was three days recovering from dehydration. We wanted to keep her. She was fast, eager, hard-working and possessed of the most beautiful build I've ever seen in one of our pups. At ten months I had begun running her now and then in double lead, where she helped me set a couple of record paces on the trapline. For two months we treated her with daily injections but she remained unhealthy and unhappy, nervous with the knowledge that Something was very wrong with her. In the end we took her out and shot her. I cried all the way home, but I think it was the best we could do for her.

With five dogs left of the eleven I had used on the Iditarod, we were ready to start building a better, stronger team, because next year Julie would run the Yukon Quest.

# 12

# THE YUKON QUEST

S o I had three good racing dogs — Sky, Rusty and Amber. I also had Comet and Streak, good work dogs but not racers. Building a race team around those three dogs in just one year seemed impossible, but Miki and I flung ourselves into preparing for the 1986 Yukon Quest with only a little trepidation.

The Yukon Quest is a young race compared to the more venerable and highly competitive Iditarod. Though touted as a thousand-mile race, I estimated the true distance to be nine hundred miles or less, while the Iditarod stretched over eleven hundred miles. That extra two hundred miles is a long, long way when you're driving a tired team. I figured the shorter, less competitive Quest might make a better first race. Besides, it runs from Whitehorse, Yukon Territory, right into our old town of Fairbanks, and it has a lower entry fee. After blowing our savings in the fateful Iditarod, Miki and I needed a cheaper race.

We had some up-and-coming puppies, and during the summer we flew to Ruby and paid $650 for a big white dog named Legs. He proved to be a determined though not necessarily reliable lead dog. Later we picked up a few more dogs in Fairbanks to fill out the team. During the winter our dogs slumped badly, just as they had the previous year, but this time they pulled out of it just before the race in a dramatic mood swing which peaked during the race. On the last training run at Kluane Lake, in Canada, the dogs acted tense and irritable from the long drive south, but as they chased the wind across the lake the tension drained away and they enjoyed the rest of the trip in the truck as we drove on into Whitehorse.

"Don't worry about the trail nor the weather nor the other racers," Miki warned me. "You're a rookie. Your worst enemies are fear, ignorance and depression." No matter that I had eleven years and some twelve thousand miles of driving dogs behind me. This race introduced a new element, stress, which I had not coped with before. I had to keep my dogs moving on the ragged edge of exhaustion. If I pushed too hard, the team would break down; if I rested too much, I'd fall behind.

I didn't have a wide selection of dogs to pick my race team from, but we did a little better than last year. I could leave behind old Loki, and Comet, who still suffered leg trouble on runs longer than sixty miles, and a couple of young dogs who didn't quite have it in them to do the race. I didn't want to bring Streak, but I needed his power. The loads carried in the sleds on the Quest are much heavier than those on the Iditarod. Up to three hundred pounds must be hauled, according to race rules, while Iditarod mushers often carry less than fifty pounds. I knew Streak couldn't go all the way, but as long as I had him I needn't worry about those big loads.

Shortly before race time we got two dogs, Stevie and

Whyley, from Fairbanks mushers to bring my race team up to nine dogs. Stevie had been run only three hundred miles that season, instead of the one or two thousand miles most trained dogs have, but he proved to be an honest, sweet-tempered dog, as tough a worker as I could ask for.

Whyley was the biggest mistake I made on the race. I dropped him at Dawson, the halfway point, and we later traded off the two-hundred-dollar dog for his weight in dog food.

My leaders, Legs and Sky, were thoroughly professional dogs. Amber and Rusty were fine team dogs. Buck, another recent addition, showed potential but I lacked confidence in him. Raven, a pup with tremendous potential, could prove too young to take the stress. Powerful, indomitable Streak rounded out my team.

Oddly, the race start didn't make any of us nervous. Miki and I felt quite gay as the nine dogs bolted from the chute. I rode the brake while Miki sat on the loaded sled, ready to give a hand in controlling the dogs on that first short dash through the crowd in downtown Whitehorse. We were the last team out, and the roaring spectators put me in a good mood. Miki slid off the sled when we hit the frozen Yukon River, leaving me alone with the dogs.

Fear, depression and ignorance. Miki had been right about that. Shortly after the race began my dogs started coming down with kennel cough, a mild though highly contagious disease comparable to the common cold in people. Though not a serious ailment, it weakens the body defenses, leaving it vulnerable to more serious infections like pneumonia if the dog is severely stressed.

Normally I'd just lay up the dogs until the coughing eased, and the danger of more serious infections would be slim. But this was a race and I couldn't stop. I didn't know how much I could safely push the dogs, and I started getting scared.

The next day Buck started staggering and dragging sporadically. I packed him for awhile, but he acted so happy and chipper I soon put him back in the team. An hour later he collapsed in a dead faint.

I was horrified. Kneeling beside the limp dog, I checked for his pulse, looked at his pale gums, palpated his abdomen. He came around in a few minutes, but I loaded him in the sled and packed him to the first checkpoint, at Carmacks. He barked eagerly the whole fifty miles, but I had him securely fastened in the sled so he couldn't jump out. I dropped him in Carmacks and there the race veterinarians confirmed my suspicion — a partial intestinal obstruction. A press plane volunteered to fly him to Fairbanks for emergency treatment.

I wanted to drop Whyley there, too. I didn't know what was wrong with him, but he wasn't helping my team at all and the next dog drop was more than two hundred miles away. If there had not been a three-dog limit on the number of animals a musher could drop before being disqualified, I certainly would have left him. But with Buck gone and Streak leaving me at the next checkpoint, I couldn't take the chance of dropping Whyley. I had to save that third chance in case one of my dogs was seriously injured. Carmacks was only the first checkpoint. I still had eight hundred miles to go.

On the next leg of the race, my team began faltering. Kennel cough made its rounds until nearly every dog had suffered from it. Most recovered in a couple days, but Rusty's cough got worse. Stevie, less trail-hardened than the others, strained his wrist on the long hills rolling through the gold country between Carmacks and Dawson City. Whyley, dehydrated and sore, began dragging. Streak's feet grew abraded and sore despite booties and ointment. Legs went off his feed.

Hanging around camp near the Stewart River, waiting for the oppressive afternoon heat to pass, I sank down to examine Streak's swollen feet again. I hated asking him to go even as far as Dawson, but I needed his power and drive. Even with the pain, his great strength carried me over the rolling hills. Streak gazed at me calmly. He didn't look unhappy at all, just glad to be resting.

Digging my fingers into his thick black ruff, I buried my head against his massive shoulder and cried, thinking of the year before. I felt I had let him down by asking him to do this again, even though he didn't seem to mind. Things weren't going that badly, really; I was traveling well, the dogs were determined despite various minor ailments, and they always rose and moved out on command. I was depressed, more from exhaustion and the fear of what might lie ahead than from any immediate difficulties.

"Up, up!" I said in the frosty silence of the night, and shook my head with amused disbelief as the tired huskies sprang up and surged forward. Legs, who always hurtled himself off the trail gasping with exhaustion when I stopped, would plunge forward at a word or even a wave of the hand. He didn't know where we were going, but he wanted to get there fast. For all the limping and coughing, they were a bunch of darned determined dogs.

"Yeah, a bunch of darn good dogs," I croaked hoarsely. "With one notable exception." As if on cue, the lagging yellow dog Whyley looked guiltily back at me. I laughed at him a little. I had never laughed at him before. I never laughed at him again.

I watched the dogs moving smoothly down the trail, their shadows sharp in the moonlight, and again I spoke, more softly this time. "This is good."

Pedaling steadily through the darkness toward the Black Hills, though, I began to feel sick. It's just a cold, I told myself. Rusty was coughing hoarsely, and I was getting scared again. I knew Whyley and Streak had to go in Dawson, and if I had to drop Rusty too, I'd be disqualified for dropping more than the limit of three dogs.

My eyes burned from sleepiness and from my head cold which, irritated by the fifteen-below night air, spread into my chest. I shut one eye, then the other, then both together, pedaling in the blind. A few minutes later, glancing up briefly to check the dogs with my beaming headlamp, I was shocked to see Amber hopping on three legs. It looked like a shoulder injury, which could knock her out of the team and me out of the race. Stopping to check her, I cleaned the snow hopefully from her feet, but I knew that wasn't the problem. She had stepped into a deep hole made by a moose hoof in the snow, and the high-speed stumble had wrenched her shoulder.

I didn't believe it — I couldn't believe it. This was Amber, fluffy, happy indestructible Amber. She never pulled hard, she never slacked off, she never got hurt nor depressed. She was always in there, her tugline taut as she floated down the trail like a cattail seed floating in the breeze.

With a mandatory thirty-six-hour layover in Dawson City, I still had a chance. I might lick this cold in my head, Stevie and Amber might heal, Rusty might recover from his cough. I pulled Amber from the team and she rode in the basket for eighty miles.

I'd heard horror stories about King Solomon's Dome, about how the trail snaked over the barren four-thousand-foot mountain and hard-packed drifts slanted down the slopes, burying the trails and often sending sleds skidding toward even steeper slopes. I listened and remembered, but I'd heard too many horror stories which didn't pan out, and I wasn't worried.

No wind nor snow threatened my way, and the dogs marched up the mountain as if it was a molehill. At the top I rested and snacked the dogs. Misty clouds glided silently past the midnight moon, casting a pall over the brilliantly lit snow.

I sat hunched tiredly on the sled, miserably sick but still fascinated by the ghostly swirls of drifted snow, the broad, windswept mountainside, the spruce-covered valley below, and the infinitely wide and glowing night sky above.

Stevie whined anxiously. Though bone tired, the gutsy little dog knew we should be going. He may not have understood the race, but he sure understood the urgency.

I howled softly to key up the dogs. They picked up the note when I dropped it, their howls rising in a powerful chorus. The concert gave the team a sense of unity, and I could feel the stress draining away as they sang. The hypnotic notes rolled down the slopes and echoed across the moonlit mountain. I listened, entranced, feeling the intense, spiritual grandness of the land around us.

After that it seemed we were traveling downhill for two hours. The long slope appeared all the longer because I held the dogs back to a trot instead of letting them lope. I was seeing a lot of minor wrist injuries and sprains, and the pounding of a long downhill lope might really do some damage.

My mind separated from my body during that trip, and I began hearing distant conversations and feeling more and more stuporous. I didn't want to stop, I just wanted to reach Dawson and die quietly for thirty-six hours.

Streak brought me back some hours later by dodging sideways toward the snow and staggering back into line. I knew he was approaching the end of his endurance. Slower than the other dogs, he'd had to lope down that long hill. When I stopped the dogs he collapsed on his side, and I found his feet had swelled up to the elbows from the constant pounding. After a few minutes he indicated that he felt up to going on, so I hiked up the dogs and gradually faded out again.

I pulled into Dawson with eight dogs, half limping, the other half coughing. Although still spirited, they were on the ragged edge of burning out completely, and they needed that mandatory rest badly. I was feeling like a zombie, but all I had to do was unhook my dogs and picket them. Race rules allowed my handler, Miki, to care for the dogs during the layover. She fed and watered them frequently, cared for their feet, tended their ills and gave them a deep bed of straw. They knew the race was not over, and they took every advantage of the rest.

I staggered away and put the race out of my mind for thirty-six hours. I slept awhile, took a bath, slept some more, and visited a dentist. The week before the race started I'd had one of my little dental disasters; punched myself in the face with an iron snow hook when the lurching dogs made my sled buck. A broken tooth had been giving me trouble, and the Dawson dentist patched it up temporarily.

When I left the small Yukon town I had just six dogs and they were all running. They were the core of my team, the best I had. But Raven and Legs were coughing, Sky and Stevie were stiff, Rusty was sneezing and Amber was still running on three cylinders as they loped down the Yukon River. I eased them back into the routine slowly, knowing they couldn't take much pressure. It cost me a couple positions in the race but kept the dogs in better shape, and in a couple of days the team came together beautifully.

I gave them a breather every hour and a snack every two hours, according to the routine our friend from Ophir, Robbie Roberts, suggested. A long rest during the afternoon saved them from running during the heat of the day, and a few hours' rest during the bitter cold of the night gave me a chance to get a hot meal into the dogs and a couple of hours' sleep for myself.

The dogs moved best at dusk. I hooked up while the day was still warm and we started sluggishly, but as it grew colder the dogs loosened up and hit a mile-eating trot just as the cold began to bite. Sometimes they moved too fast, and I was afraid they would burn out my pup, Raven. She kept pulling, but the speed wore her out and when her pace grew ragged I'd stop and snack the dogs, hoping full stomachs might slow them down a little.

Woodchopper, on the Yukon River, looked deserted but for the bright lantern shining in the window. Inside, the cabin glowed with warmth from the barrel stove. I found hot water, coffee and cocoa laid out. No one was there.

The Yukon Quest had many silent benefactors — trail-breakers, ham radio operators, vets, organizers, checkers, sponsors, and the many people along the way who simply wanted to help each weary musher any way they could. From the free meal at Crabb's Corner in Central and the gas-station lady's generosity at 101-Mile Steese Highway, to the wonderful people at Stepping Stone and Maisy May in Canada, the same generous hospitality was given.

At Woodchopper I fed my dogs, left them to rest, and slipped into the roadhouse to savor a few hours of warmth and solitude. It was the only time during the race that I really felt secure. In the dark hours before dawn I roused the dogs and left. I never saw anyone.

We arrived at Circle City, two hundred miles from Fairbanks, after dark the next evening. Returning to mankind after more than a hundred-fifty miles of Yukon River solitude made me feel giddy. I fed my dogs, treated their worn feet, helped with the vet exam, gave them straw, and then tottered into the community building for a snack and a nap. Inside, I had the weird experience of watching Joe Runyan, in Fairbanks, win the Yukon Quest on satellite TV.

Eagle Summit yields horror stories just as King Solomon Dome does, but the trail runs on the Steese Highway so I knew the grade must be shallow, and with good weather I had nothing to fear despite the intense blackness of the night.

At the top I loaded Raven into the sled. She had started

acting goofy, an early sign of burnout, and I wanted her to rest before making the last dash from the Chena Hot Springs checkpoint into Fairbanks.

Half a mile over the crest, Legs decided to take a rest. He didn't quit often, only three times during the fourteen-day race, and I trusted his judgment. Usually he just darted off the trail and flopped down to rest for a few minutes. This time, when he darted off the trail he found himself in midair. He had plunged off a thirty-foot embankment.

His weight dragged the other dogs over behind him. I stopped the sled inches from the sheer edge of the highway, with the team hanging against their harnesses below. The icy pavement offered no anchor for my snow hook, and I broke into a hot sweat as the sled inched over the drop-off.

Feverishly releasing Raven's restraining ropes, I pushed the young dog off the sled. If I went over with her secured on top of my load, the rolling sled might injure her.

"Legs, Sky," I called softly. "Come gee — easy —"

I didn't see how they could climb back up, but I didn't know what else to do. It took all my strength just to keep the sled from tumbling over.

The dogs shifted in response to my command and the gentle tug on the towline pulled me over the edge. Musher, sled and dogs hurtled down the embankment. We cartwheeled, rolled and skidded down the steep slope, and at last came to a precarious stop against a small rock.

The long beam of my headlamp flashed over the dogs and then down the snow-packed slope. I couldn't see the bottom. Even as I reconnoitered, the sled began sliding again. Gasping, I set the hook into the icy slope to keep the outfit from gliding on down into the abyss. Then came the sweat-popping chore of climbing back to the road. I unloaded the sled and dragged the dogs, slipping and struggling, back up the near cliff to the road, and then ferried my load up the slippery slope and repacked it. The job left me utterly exhausted.

I grabbed Legs by the ears. "I'll never forgive you for this, dog!"

The last mountain before Chena Hot Springs was a killer, mostly because we were so tired. My dogs caught up with our friend and fellow racer, Patty Doval, and I followed her into the last checkpoint, but I didn't leave with her. The eighteen-hour pull from the previous checkpoint left my small team exhausted. Also, by leaving two hours later than Patty, I avoided traveling during the sweltering afternoon hours when the temperature soared above freezing. I may have missed a chance at coming in nineteenth or even eighteenth instead of twentieth, but the dogs really needed that extra two hours' rest and so did I.

My dogs had gone over the last seventy miles of trail, right into downtown Fairbanks, on an earlier training run. When they recognized the trail they went berserk. Legs, always a take'em-home dog, set a pace I doubted the dogs could hold for more than a few miles. Raven, so tired, now bounced and giggled and played with her running mate at every stop. Stevie didn't want to stop at all, and neither did Legs. They started yelping and harness-banging like fresh sprint dogs at every stop.

For once I didn't slow the dogs down when they moved too fast. I gave Legs his head and let them go. But just like clockwork, I kept up the routine I had held for the two weeks of the race. An hour running, a breather. Another hour running, a snack.

At first the dogs didn't want to stop, much less rest, but after twenty miles the speed got to them. They kept going, but at every pause Legs toppled on his side, only to spring up and charge forward when I said "Up, up." Every two hours I poured food into them, hoping to keep them going. If it had been a race to the finish, my pace would have been really exciting, but the truth is I hardly ever saw the other racers. The competitive mushers were far ahead of me, and the "campers" were far behind.

Two miles from the finish line Legs plunged off the trail, apparently intending to quit. Mushers had actually scratched this close to a finish line, and with the dogs this tipsy I had to be careful. I let Legs go.

The powerful white dog didn't stop in the deep snow, as he usually did. He plowed through the chest-deep snow halfway across the Chena River, dragging the confused team behind him. Then he paused to lift his leg on a tree frozen in the ice. I waited. Give him five minutes, he'll go — I hope.

But he didn't take five minutes. He finished his business and charged back to the trail, the reluctant team floundering after him.

"OK, Legs, I forgive you." Gliding under the glowing Fairbanks bridges that span the Chena, I watched my team with pride. Despite sickness and injury, they had hung together with a staunch determination that never failed me. Unlike the Iditarod team the previous year, this team had the attitude for racing, and that made all the difference.

It was 4:30 a.m. As we approached the finish line, I sang out "Hike, hike!" For the first time on the whole race I was asking the dogs to move faster. "Up, up!"

The dogs broke out of their swift trot and loped across the line.

I really had no fun at all on the race. The start and the finish were the only really good times. Yet despite the gloom that followed me along the trail, once the trip was over the memories left me with a strong feeling of pride, satisfaction and, for some reason, joy. As in our first long trip through Denali Park, the worst adventures make the best memories.

## 13

# TRAILS TO THE FUTURE

The gas lantern outside the cabin gave a cheerful glow, valiantly opening a small spot of light in the vast blackness of the early Alaskan morning. I tied down the last rope on the dogsled, lashing the load securely in place, and glanced at my watch. Seven-thirty. I was ready, the dogs were ready. Julie stood near the door of Birch Cabin, drenched in the light of the lantern.

"Hike!"

My six big sled-dogs shot forward with a breath-catching surge of power. The sled bounced off a tree or two in the narrow trail, and then we were off, rushing through the darkness. The dogs loped for two miles and then slowed to a steady, conservative trot.

Two hours later the sky began to lighten, casting the scrubby spruce trees and snow in a faint gray, gradually turning to a pale blue until finally, at ten-thirty, the sun crept over the rim of the mountain, touching the trees with gold. My spirits rose with the far-off ball of fire.

I was heading to the Spruce Cabin, twenty-seven miles away. The dogs trotted easily, traveling six miles an hour despite the three inches of fresh snow and the windblown trail. Stopping to bait the marten traps slowed our progress, however, and when the sun rose we had reached the creek, only fifteen miles out, which we would follow the remaining twelve miles to the cabin.

The first three miles often have open holes, and despite the ten-below weather they had holes today. Nearly every bend sported a stretch of open water, rushing and sparkling three inches deep over the cobbles and pebbles. The dogs, used to it, trotted right through the water when the trail crossed the current to the other side, and even I didn't mind getting wet in the relatively warm weather.

I did mind how fast the sky was clearing after that blizzard last night, with its ominous north wind and gritty, swirling snow. Now in the calm stillness I realized this must be a cold front pushing in, and in early January we could expect our harshest temperatures.

Once past the tricky stretch, the creek was safe. In the open areas the dogs plowed through six to eight inches of drifted snow and their rate slowed to three or four miles an hour. I pedaled and walked, easing their burden. I didn't have to tell Loki to stop at the sets. He knew them as well as I did, and always looked hopefully to see whether I'd caught anything. The stench of rotten fish bait permeated my gloves, but the reeking odor had long since become a part of life.

The cabin, cold and dark, looked just like home as I helped the team haul the loaded sled up the steep bank of the creek. Small, with walls of big spruce logs, it would be toasty warm soon after I lit the wood stove, and glad I was; the temperature had been dropping all day.

A frigid gush of thirty-below air greeted me the following morning as I opened the door. I breathed deeply, feeling the tiny hairs in my nose freeze together with an odd prickly sensation. The dogs welcomed my appearance eagerly, and despite the cold they did not mind as I hooked them up for the run through the hills on the Grayling Creek trail. I added two more marten to the three I'd caught the day before, and although the air grew warmer as I climbed to tree line, I eyed the sharply clear sky warily. All around me the low, rolling hills spread out, only two thousand feet above sea level yet eighteen thousand feet below the crest of Denali, just twenty miles away.

Let me be conservative and say this is a marvelous land! Let me make an understatement and say the wonder of it is beyond belief, that those who have not stood here can never imagine the power of it all. Here in its presence the Mountain is overpowering, whether dominating the land in shimmering moonlit glory or withdrawn behind a veil of restless clouds. Even when the Mountain lies hidden the land is grand, the hills with their scattering of battered, tiny, snow-drenched spruce, the gray fog pressing and dense, the slopes twisted and contorted, cut by stunted drainages and dotted with tiny, frozen ponds. And when the Mountain stands clear, overwhelming large and small beneath it, I can pause on the edge of the highest ridge, close my eyes, stretch out my hands and touch the face of Wickersham Wall.

By the next morning the temperature had fallen to forty below. I spent the day snowshoeing out another sideline, trying to find the trail. We'd never trapped that way and weren't sure where Slim's old trail ran. Once out in the loose scrub-spruce, I lost the trail and meandered back and forth across the countryside in vain. Darkness would be falling soon, and an odd haze already obscured the sun.

I hit an overflowed creek and followed it, snowshoeing easily over ice covering fresh water over the original ice, instead of plowing through the three feet of snow blanketing the surrounding land. But as I crossed a small patch of snow I suddenly felt myself sinking. I knew I had hit fresh overflow, insulated by the snow and not yet hardened despite the cold. I couldn't back up in the snowshoes, so I slipped my feet from the simple toe bindings and leaped off them, back as far as I could toward firm ice, aiming for a spot where the water looked only a half-inch thick. But when I landed the young ice broke, and instantly I was in ankle-deep water.

At forty below I knew I could be in real trouble, especially with a grievous shortage of nearby firewood. Another leap carried me out of the slushy water and quickly I rubbed my fur mukluks in the soft snow on the creek bank. The powder absorbed most of the water and my feet inside stayed warm and fairly dry. Retrieving the snowshoes with a long stick, I banged off the freezing slush and cut up the bank, heading back toward the cabin, relieved to have escaped so easily.

During the night the temperature continued to fall, down to fifty degrees below zero. When I came out to the clear, dim morning the cold took my breath away. At fifty below the air feels thick and sticks in your throat, choking you when you take a deep breath, and I could hear the condensation in my breath freezing with a soft, crinkly hiss.

Usually we do not travel at these temperatures. The smallest incident can lead to frostbite; a minor injury can lead to death. Cheeks and exposed flesh freeze if care is not taken, especially with the breeze created by moving.

But with a limited amount of dog food and Julie worrying about me at the other cabin, I knew I ought to try to get home. The way this cold front moved in, I figured it would be here for days. I might as well go now and save Julie some worry, as wait for two days until I ran out of food and still end up traveling at fifty below. I didn't have overmitts with me, so I stuffed dry grass into my mittens and still-damp mukluks for extra insulation.

The dogs knew they were going home. They bolted down the trail before I was fairly on the runners and I let them go, knowing they would quickly settle down, pacing themselves in the bitter cold. My thick parka ruff warded off most of the breeze, and I pedaled steadily as the team headed for home.

Condensation from the dogs' breath hung in a fog bank over their backs, coating the thick fur a frosty white, leaving lines where the harness webbing covered the hairs. Each of the twenty-four feet clipped along, landing quickly and surely with a small puff of snow, and the only sounds were the rush of the runners, the crunch of snow beneath my pedaling foot, and the occasional jingle of a harness snap.

Thoughts become diffuse; dreams mingle with the fog. Trapping — you have to love it, or you would hate it. For now, it's enough. What does the future hold? Who knows? I try not to think of the influx of population, of trapline encroachers, of fly-in trap-robbers, or recreationists taking over our — Slim's — trails and cabins. I live each day as it comes, gleaning every moment offered, filling them with work and adventure, with thoughts and dreams. What next? Maybe I'll run the Iditarod again, if they don't make the rules too tough for the rinky-dink dog musher. And if I do, Julie gets to, too. How about mushing from Skagway to Fairbanks? Or a trip up north, or to Southwestern Alaska?

No, let's think big! The day is long, the trail is slow; we have time to dream big dreams. Let's mush across the Bering Strait to Siberia! Better yet, go over there and follow the Trans-Siberian Railroad clear to Europe. Holy Smokes, this is getting exciting! Now I have it — yes — a circumpolar expedition by dog team, following the Arctic Circle, a two-girl-nine-dog embassy of friendship and adventure. Siberia, Russia, Finland, Norway, Greenland, Canada, and — best of all — *Alaska*. Not wild enough? All right, let's head south and follow Sir Robert Scott's tracks to the South Pole, using dogs as he did but substituting reindeer for the ponies! Never mind how a couple of two-bit trappers on a four-bit trapline could afford to support such dreams — sometimes it is the dreams that support the trappers.

The twenty-seven miles seemed especially long, but at least the creek had frozen solid. I spied only one small patch of open water, just inches in diameter, which the sled runner passed over easily. Wet feet at this temperature would mean either stopping to build a fire or risking frostbite.

The sun slipped away in the early afternoon, and the light drained off over the next two hours. By five-thirty the dogs were feeling their way down the trail in pitch blackness, only the stars giving off diminutive dots of light. The team pulled steadily, silently, possessed only by the thought of reaching home. My cheeks and hands grew cold, but not painfully cold. Only my legs, unprotected by overpants, bothered me, and even they were not dangerously cold.

The South Pole is an awfully long way away, isn't it? Cold, too, and windy. And it's an awfully long way around the world when you're traveling seven miles an hour. With the darkness the dreams shrink to more manageable sizes. Maybe . . . maybe we should just buy a couple Icelandic horses and let it go at that.

The tiny pinprick of lantern light shone through the window of the cabin, warming my heart as it peeked through the trees. The dogs began to run and I gave them an encouraging shout. In another moment I would be inside the cabin, surrounded by panting dogs, bright light, the warmth of the roaring wood stove and Julie's questions. Another trip on the trapline was finished, and I was glad to be home.

Many other fascinating books are available from
ALASKA NORTHWEST BOOKS™
Ask for them at your favorite bookstore,
or write us for a free catalog.

ALASKA NORTHWEST BOOKS™
A division of GTE Discovery Publications, Inc.
130 Second Avenue South
Edmonds, WA 98020

Or call toll-free 1-800-331-3510